JOHN WASZEK was educated at St. Joseph's College, Stoke on Trent and obtained his degree in Economics at the City University, London before undertaking post-graduate studies at Loughborough College of Education. At present he is Head of Economics and Business Studies at Hedingham School, Essex.

GCE O-Level Passbooks

CHEMISTRY, C. W. Laphan, M.Sc.

COMPUTER STUDIES, R. J. Bradley, B.Sc.

MODERN MATHEMATICS, A. J. Sly, B.A.

HISTORY (*Social and Economic,* 1815–1951), M. C. James, B.A.

HISTORY (*Political and Constitutional*), 1815–1951, L. James, B.A., M.Litt.

HUMAN BIOLOGY, S. Cantle, B.Sc., M.Med.Sci.

FRENCH, G. Butler, B.A.

ENGLISH LANGUAGE, Robert L. Wilson, M.A.

BIOLOGY, R. Whitaker, B.Sc., and

J. M. Kelly, B.Sc., M.I.Biol.

PHYSICS, B. P. Brindle, B.Sc.

ECONOMICS, J. E. Waszek, B.Sc. (Econ)

GEOGRAPHY (*British Isles*), R. Bryant, B.A., and R. Knowles, M.A.

TECHNICAL DRAWING, P. Barnett, D.S.C., M.C.C. Ed., Adv. Dip. Ed.

GCE O-Level Passbook

Economics

J. E. Waszek, B.Sc. (Econ.)

Published by Charles Letts & Co Ltd
London, Edinburgh and New York

First published 1980 by Intercontinental Book Productions

Published 1983 by Charles Letts & Co Ltd
Diary House, Borough Road, London SE1 1DW

2nd edition 1st impression 9.82.15

Made and printed by Charles Letts (Scotland) Ltd
ISBN 0 85097 540 9

Contents

Introduction

This book has been designed for students studying GCE O-level and CSE economics, and in the preparation of the contents due consideration has been made of the syllabuses and recent examination papers of the relevant boards. The book provides a common core of all economics syllabuses, together with some topics which appear only on certain syllabuses.

The book considers both the descriptive and analytical aspects of the subject. However the student of economics must also be able to support any assertions with up-to-date information, and it is with this in mind that a large quantity of the most recently available statistics are included, both in the figures and tables, and within the text. The student should not underestimate the importance of supporting any work with examples and statistical information.

The style and content of economics examination papers varies between examining boards. Some set an essay paper, others include a paper of multiple choice questions. Also the emphasis and style of the questions varies from board to board, so you are advised to examine the syllabus that you are taking, and consult some past papers of the board concerned. The section on examination hints (pages 188 to 194 inclusive), includes some actual examination questions, and the addresses of all the GCE and CSE examining boards, from where you can obtain the syllabus, and normally some past papers.

Acknowledgements

I am most grateful to The Controller of Her Majesty's Stationery Office for permission to reproduce the following copyright material:

Figure 8, Figure 27 and Figure 28 from *Britain 1982: An Official Handbook.*
Table 14, Table 25, Table 32 and Table 39 from *Britain 1982: An Official Handbook.*
Figure 10 from *Social Trends 1979.*
Table 30, Table 31 and Table 32 from *Annual Abstract of Statistics.*

Chapter 1
Introducing Economics

In 1776 Adam Smith, in his famous book '*The Wealth of Nations*' defined economics as what it was that caused nations to become wealthy. Alfred Marshall described the subject as 'the study of mankind in the everyday business of life'. Lord Keynes, writing in the 1930s saw economics as a toolbox, from which people took out particular tools in order to tackle particular problems. A generally acceptable definition of economics is that it is the study of how man uses the various economic resources at his disposal to produce goods and services with which he can satisfy his needs and wants.

The economic problem

All human communities encounter a common economic problem. Each community has certain resources which will enable it to produce goods and services. It will have land and raw materials such as minerals, trees and crops; it will have a supply of tools (termed capital goods), which will aid in the productive process. These tools might be very simple, such as a hammer and chisel, or very complex, such as a nuclear power station. The community will also have a supply of labour who can use the tools to help turn the raw materials into a finished product. Thus the community's economic resources consist of natural resources (land and raw materials), capital goods and labour.

The community will also have certain material needs and demands which will have to be satisfied. Clearly each person will need a supply of water, food and clothing simply to live. However the community may wish for other things such as televisions, furniture, hospitals and schools.

All societies will discover that their demand for goods and services will almost certainly exceed their ability to produce – which is determined by their economic resources; this situation is referred to as the economic problem.

A society faced by the basic economic problem must therefore indulge in the process of choosing which demands to fulfill, and which demands will have to go unsatisfied. For example, a country at war may demand armaments to fight with, and consumer goods for those at home; a choice has to be made and it is likely that it will be made in favour of armaments and against consumer goods. This is referred to as the problem of choice.

In making a choice between competing demands, a decision concerning production is being made. In the case of the war-time economy described above the decision is made to produce armaments but not to produce consumer goods. In fact there are four other production decisions that the community will have to make concerning the allocation of the existing resources between the competing demands. The five production decisions are:–

1. What to produce? Should the community produce armaments or consumer goods?

2. How much to produce? Should the community produce a small number of armaments and many consumer goods or, a large number of armaments and a few consumer goods?

3. How to produce? Should the armaments and consumer goods be produced in large fully automated factories or in small workshops by highly skilled men and women? The second method would probably involve the production of higher quality goods.

4. For whom to produce? Should the consumer goods be produced for those people who have nothing, for those people who already have consumer goods, or for those who can afford to buy them?

5. Where to produce? Should goods be produced where the costs of production are lowest, or where unemployment is very high?

The problem of choice can be illustrated by the use of a production possibility curve, an example is shown in Figure 1, below.

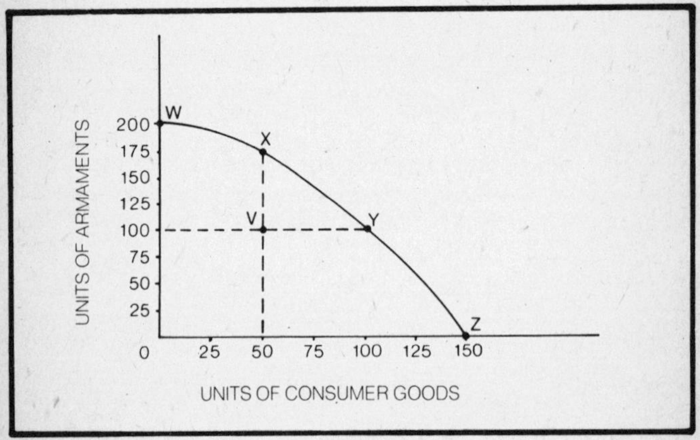

Figure 1. A production possibility curve

If it is assumed that a community produces only two types of good, consumer goods and armaments. Units of consumer goods which can be produced are plotted on the vertical axis, and units of armaments which can be produced are plotted on the horizontal axis. If the community uses all available resources it can produce at any point on the production possibility curve (WZ), i.e. the community could choose point W, where 200 units of armaments and no consumer goods will be produced; alternatively it could choose point X (175 units of armaments, 50 units of consumer goods), point Y (100 armaments, 100 consumer goods). or point Z (no armaments, 150 consumer goods). If the community produced at point V, inside the production possibility curve (50 consumer goods, 100 armaments), then it is failing to use all its economic resources, for if it did so it could produce either an extra 75 units of armaments or an extra 50 units of consumer goods. The community will be unable to produce at a point outside the curve, as the curve shows the production possibilities with the given level of resources. The only way in which it will be able to reach such a point will be by increasing its resources, which will enable the community to produce more of both goods, i.e. the production possibility curve will move outwards from the origin. Such a movement is illustrated in Figure 2, below.

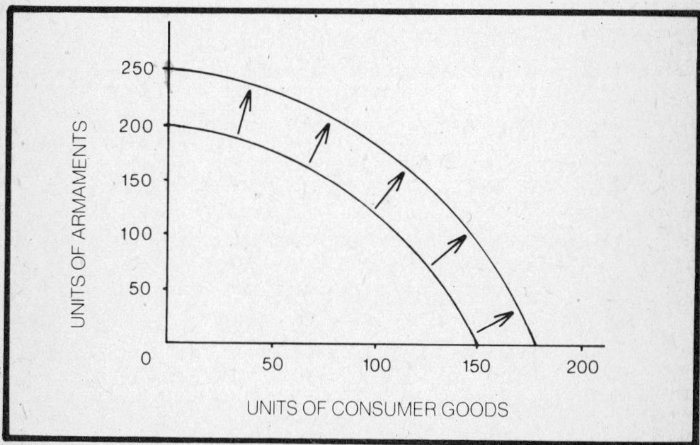

Figure 2. The effect of an increase in a community's economic resources

Opportunity Cost

Opportunity cost is an important economic concept, and can be explained with the use of a simple example. Suppose a government decides to build a new road at a cost of £5 millions. However, the alternative was to use this finance to build a new hospital. Thus, although the money cost of the road is £5 millions, the opportunity cost of the road is one new hospital, because by building the new road the community has foregone the opportunity of its alternative – a new hospital.

Opportunity cost is therefore the cost of something in terms of the value of the next best alternatives which have to be foregone to obtain it.

The production possibility curve in Figure 1 can also be used to illustrate the concept of opportunity cost. If the community is operating at point Y (100 armaments, 100 consumer goods), and it wishes to produce an extra 75 units of armaments because it is now involved in a war, then it will have to move to point X, where it can produce 175 units of armaments and 50 units of consumer goods. Thus the opportunity cost of 75 extra units of armaments is the 50 units of consumer goods which will have to be foregone.

Economic systems

A community has, therefore, several important decisions to make about production and may use the production possibility curve and the concept of opportunity cost to aid decision making. The community will have to formulate a method to establish how the decisions are to be made concerning the allocation of the available resources. In theory there are two basic systems which can be utilized to make production decisions. The market economy allows decisions to be made by private individuals working through a price system; in the planned economy production decisions are made by government planning agencies. However, most countries fall under neither of these headings as some decisions regarding the allocation of resources are made through a price system, whereas others are made by planning agencies. This type of system is called the mixed economy.

These three systems are examined in detail below.

1. The market economy

In the market economy resources are privately owned and production decisions are made by private individuals and private firms acting in their own self-interest, in response to the forces of supply and demand. If a firm is producing a good which people wish to buy, that firm will purchase various resources such as raw materials, machinery and labour. Thus consumers are directly influencing the quantity of resources given to the production of that good. If demand for the good rises the firm will increase output to obtain higher profits, and in the process will employ more resources. If demand falls, the firm will reduce output and reduce the quantity of resources that it uses. Generally, those firms which produce the goods which people wish to buy will earn a profit, whereas those firms which produce goods and services that people do not wish to buy will make a loss, and subsequently curtail production.

It is in this way that production decisions are made in the market economy. It is through the market mechanism the production decisions will be made. Firms, like individuals, will act in their own self-interest and will decide the production method and the location which will ensure the highest possible profits. Certain advantages are claimed to accompany the market economy.

1. Private individuals have the economic freedom to buy and sell as they wish. They can own property, enter into contracts, offer their services to an employer, lend money at interest and rent property.
2. There is no need for government bureaucracy and red-tape.
3. Competition between firms will encourage low prices, economic efficiency, the innovation of new processes and the invention of new products.
4. The prospects of personal rewards for effort and initiative will encourage individuals to work hard, and be successful.
5. Only those goods required by consumers will be produced.

However the market economy has certain disadvantages.

1. An unequal distribution of income usually exists under such a system, and this means that some individuals will have more economic freedom than others. Furthermore, poorer people may be unable to purchase goods that they need to live but cannot afford, e.g. food, clothing, housing, medical services.
2. Sellers tend to combine into monopolies or come to mutually beneficial agreements which enable them to keep prices high and/or keep wages low.
3. Wasteful competition may occur in certain markets.
4. External costs and benefits will not be taken into account; for example, if a firm pollutes the atmosphere with smoke, the extra cost of washing clothes neccesitated by dirt in the air is the responsibility of the firm – but those suffering from the pollution will find it very difficult, if not impossible, to reclaim these costs from the firm.
5. Public goods (see Chapter 16) will not be produced.

2. The planned economy

In the planned economy production decisions are made by state planning authorities guided by social preferences rather than consumers' demands. To make its planning decisions effective the state normally owns the means of production and distribution, i.e. all production is state controlled. The main advantages of this system are as follows:–

1. Goods can be produced on the basis of need rather than effective demand, i.e. desire to buy something backed by the willingness and ability to pay for it.
2. The state can plan spending so as to ensure that the productive capacity of the nation increases, i.e. it can plan for more power stations and less chocolate factories.
3. The state can ensure that everyone is employed by running parts of industry at a loss.
4. Wasteful competition will not exist.

The main disadvantages of the planned economy are:–

1. Planners may be inefficient in the sense that they do not correctly estimate the needs of the people, causing shortages of some goods and large unwanted stocks of others.
2. So as to build up the country's productive potential, planners may unduly depress the current standard of living, e.g. too few consumers' goods are produced and too many factories and machines.
3. Planners are less likely to take the risks involved with the introduction of new products, or new production techniques.
4. Personal freedom may be reduced if state planning becomes too detailed, and individuals have to live their lives in step with an overall economic plan.

3. The mixed economy

Many countries, including the United Kingdom and her partners in the European Economic Community (EEC), the United States of America (USA) and Canada have mixed economies. This system attempts to obtain the benefits of both the market and the planned economies, and the disadvantages of neither. As a result there is considerable government intervention in what is basically a private enterprise (market) economy. The ability to own private property is seen as an important facet of the mixed economy, it is claimed that this provides an incentive for people to work and save. The main areas of government activity in the mixed economy (specifically in the UK) are discussed in detail in Chapter 16), and are listed on the next page.

1. The provision of public goods, such as law and order and defence.
2. The provision of social welfare schemes to ensure that basic needs, such as medical care and education can be obtained regardless of the ability to pay.
3. The supervision of private industry to prevent the occurence of unfair trade practices as might be created by monopolies or cartels.
4. The production of goods and services, through nationalized industries, which private industry is unwilling to supply due to high risks or high costs, such as nuclear power stations.
5. The control of the economy by various methods, to attempt to prevent, or alleviate the problems associated with inflation, high unemployment, or a low level of economic growth – where the productive capacity of the nation is growing too slowly.

Key terms

Economics is the study of how man allocates the available resources amongst competing demands.
The Economic problem refers to the excess of needs and demands over the means to satisfy these wants.
Production possibility curves show the level of output that a community can obtain with a given level of economic resources.
Opportunity cost is the cost of something expressed in terms of the next best alternatives foregone.
The production decisions are: What to produce? How much to produce? How to produce? For whom to produce? Where to produce?
In a **market economy** the production decisions are made by private individuals and firms through a price system.
In a **planned economy** the production decisions are made by state planning authorities.
In a **mixed economy** some decisions are made by state planning agencies, and others are made by individuals and firms through a price system.

Chapter 2
Factors of Production

Production

The word production usually refers to the act of making or creating something. A car worker, a bricklayer or a toolmaker is considered to be productive and is therefore taking part in production, whereas a solicitor, a roadsweeper or a shop assistant might not normally be considered to be productive as none of them actually makes anything. In economics, production refers to the process of fulfilling wants, regardless of whether anything is created, and thus all those who are involved in satisfying wants are productive. On this basis the solicitor is productive because individuals and organizations are prepared to pay him to satisfy their wants, whether this is drawing up a contract or representing them in court; the roadsweeper is productive because the community, acting through their local council are prepared to pay him to satisfy their wants, cleaner streets; the shop assistant is also productive because without his labour no-one would be able to satisfy their wants by buying goods. Therefore all persons who are paid to satisfy economic wants by producing goods and providing services are productive, and are involved in production.

The output of goods and services can be classified into three groups.

1. Consumer goods, which consist of

(a) *Non-durable consumer goods;* these have a relatively short life or are consumed in the act of being used. Food, clothing, coal, petrol and light bulbs are examples.

(b) *Durable consumer goods;* these usually have a much longer life, examples include furniture, motor cars, household electrical appliances.

2. Capital goods (also referred to as 'producer' goods). These goods aid in the production of other goods and are used by producers. Unlike consumer goods they are not purchased for the satisfaction that they give to the purchaser, but for their ability to help produce other goods. Tools, machines, blast furnaces and lorries are all examples.

3. Services. These are mainly intangible things and are often consumed at the same time as they are produced, such as a telephone call, postal services, and the advice of a solicitor or an accountant. Services are consumed by consumers to fulfill wants and also by producers to aid in the productive process.

Factors of production

All productive processes require certain economic resources before they can proceed, these resources are called factors of production and are classified under the four headings of Land, Labour, Capital and Enterprise.

A simple example can illustrate the importance of each of these factors. The potter needs clay; glazes; a potter's wheel; a kiln; he will also have to organize the running of his pottery and take the risk that he may lose everything if no-one wants to buy the pots he makes.

The resources that the potter has used can be classified under the four headings.
Land (which also refers to Natural Resources): clay, glazes.
Labour: his own physical efforts of making the pots, and the mental effort of organizing the pottery.
Capital: the potter's wheel, the kiln.
Enterprise: the risk that he may lose everything if no-one wants to buy his pots.

All productive processes contain an element of each of these factors, although it is sometimes difficult to classify some things under one of the headings. It is important to examine each factor of production in detail, and this is done below.

Land

The factor of production Land is the term used to describe all natural resources available to man which are gifts of nature. In referring to land the economist includes land and fertility of the soil, forests, grass, crops, minerals, sunshine, rainfall, temperature, seas and rivers, animals, birds, fish and so on.

The supply of natural resources

Some natural resources can be increased in quantity by application of the other factors of production. The world can produce more meat by raising more animals, more wood by planting more trees, and more wheat by sowing more corn. However, many natural resources are limited in supply, and mankind is unable to ignore the threat that one day there will be no minerals left to mine. Some minerals, tin and copper, for instance, are already scarce, and that vital commodity oil is expected to run out within thirty years.

The mobility of land

Land is geographically immobile, Mount Everest cannot be moved to some other geographical location; but whilst some land may be useful for just one activity, land is generally mobile in the sense that it is capable of more than one use. Commercial considerations will determine the use of a particular piece of land, unless the government decides that in the interests of society as a whole, a piece of land should or should not be used for a particular purpose.

The geographical immobility of land determines the land's value. In town centres, the area of land is limited and cannot be increased regardless of the demand for it, and there will be a tendency for its value to rise.

The law of diminishing returns

The early economists perceived that as additional units of the variable factor, labour, were used with a fixed quantity of land, a point would be reached when the returns coming from the variable factor would decline. Returns here means the output derived from the factor of production. For example, a farmer employs an agricultural labourer to grow wheat on a large field. After a year the farmer decides to employ a second labourer to try and increase the output of wheat. After a second year the farmer takes on a third labourer. Each year the farmer employs an extra labourer and measures the total output of wheat from the field, with the following results:

Number of labourers	Total output (bushels)	Output of extra labourer
1	10	10
2	22	12
3	38	16
4	46	8
5	50	4
6	47	−3

With one labourer output is only 10 bushels because he has too little time to perform all the tasks required of him. The introduction of the second labourer enables the two men to divide up the work and raise total output. With three men each can specialize on what he does best and total output rises substantially. However the introduction of the fourth and fifth increases production by a small amount because the men find there are so many of them on one field that sometimes there is nothing for them to do. The hiring of the sixth worker actually reduces production because there are now too many labourers and they get in each others way. If a seventh man were employed the problem would become even more severe.

Initially the farmer gained increasing returns from employing more men, but after a point (3 labourers) additional units of labour increased production by a diminishing amount and eventually total output declined with the hiring of an extra worker. Thus, the growing of wheat on the field is subject to diminishing returns if four or more labourers are employed.

Originally, the law of diminishing returns was considered to be specially relevant to land, but it is now clear that it can apply to all the factors of production.

Labour

Labour is an important factor of production and consists of the human resources which are available to take part in production. Labour cannot be owned like other factors of production, Land and Capital, rather it is the services of labour which have to be purchased. Labour is very different in many other ways to the other factors of production and is considered in more detail.

The supply of labour

A nation's total supply of labour is that proportion of the population who are able and willing to work, defined as the working population. The working population of the U.K. as at March 1982 is given below.

Status	Millions
Employees in employment	21·1
Employers and self-employed	1·9
Unemployed	3·0
Armed forces	0·3
Total working population	26·3

Table 1. The working population (March 1982)

The working population is considered in detail in Chapter 8. The size of the working population is basically determined by the proportion of the population who are in the working-age group (men 16 to 65, women 16 to 60), and the numbers in the working age group who cannot work or who do not offer themselves for employment – mainly students in full time education and housewifes. It is important to note that those who are registered as unemployed are part of the working population, and form part of the labour supply, as they would be in employment if suitable work could be found for them.

The efficiency of labour

A nation's ability to produce goods and services is not only limited by the supply of labour but also the quality of the labour available.

1. Education and skill

It is generally believed that higher levels of production are attainable with a skilled, well educated workforce. Consider the difficulties experienced in some developing nations where even some of the most simple production techniques cannot be used because the population is illiterate and innumerate. However, if a nation wishes to increase its productive potential, training establishments must teach workers the skills industry requires.

2. Health and welfare

Each year Britain loses about 400 million to 500 million working days through illness, over forty times the number of days lost, in an average year through strikes. Clearly a more healthy workforce will be a more efficient one. Spending on the National Health Service, therefore, not only reduces personal misery, but increases the productive potential of the nation.

3. Working conditions

Poor working conditions invariably lead to low productivity. If a worker is too hot or too cold, or has unpleasant surroundings his output will fall. Conditions in places of work must by law be of a minimum standard, and the Factory Inspectorate ensures that employers comply with the regulations. The majority of firms now accept the need to provide good working conditions to encourage high productivity amongst their workers.

4. Motivation

The motivation of labour will affect its efficiency. The introduction of assembly line methods have brought boredom and monotony to many workers, the nature of the work gives little satisfaction and this may result in a lack of motivation. Some firms have brought in bonus payments and profit sharing schemes in an attempt to increase workers' motivation, and recent developments suggest that schemes of this type will increase in number.

The mobility of labour

Labour tends to be both occupationally and geographically immobile. Although nearly two million people change their job each year, they are frequently obtaining similar employment in different firms. The occupational immobility of labour leads to problems for both firms and workers. Firms experience a shortage of workers with certain skills, holding back production. For example in September 1978 there were 125 vacancies for every 100 unemployed toolmakers and fitters. At the same time some workers are unable to obtain employment because in their occupation the number of unemployed exceeds the number of vacancies. If labour were more occupationally mobile, production would increase and unemployment would fall. **The main causes of occupational immobility are:**

1. A lack of inherent skill and intelligence, which is required for certain occupations e.g. few people have the ability to become a surgeon.
2. The cost and length of training.
3. Discrimination on the grounds of sex, age, marital status, colour, race or creed.
4. Ignorance of opportunities available.
5. Restrictive practices by trade unions, who may insist on, for example, a five year apprenticeship.

Labour is also geographically immobile, although immobility of this type varies with income. Higher income groups tend to be more mobile than lower income groups. This is almost certainly due to the financial cost of moving, which is one of the major factors limiting geographical mobility. **The main causes of geographical immobility are:**

1. The cost of moving home. Those on higher incomes, who have skills which are in greater demand often find that employers are prepared to pay certain removal expenses.
2. The cost and availability of housing. In some areas, especially London and the South East, houses are in short supply and are also more expensive than in other parts of the country.
3. Social ties.
4. Family ties.
5. Ignorance of opportunities.
6. Some people have a prejudice against living in certain parts of the country.

Geographical immobility causes labour shortages in certain areas, particularly the South East, and also causes unemployment, particularly in the North, Wales and Scotland.

The division of labour

In primitive societies man is obliged to procure the necessities of life for himself. When he learns to cooperate with his fellows each man can specialize in the production of those goods for which he has the greatest aptitude. The total output of all goods will increase and each man can exchange his surplus with that of others. This specialization of labour is more commonly termed the division of labour.

In a modern society specialization between workers is practised to an extreme degree. In a factory a man may spend all his time on a straightforward process which forms only a small part of a complex production process.

The first writings on the effect that the division of labour could have on output were by Adam Smith, in his book '*The Wealth of Nations*'; published in 1776. Smith visited a pin making factory and found that if one man performed all the processes required to make a pin, then he would normally produce about 20 pins each day. However, the firm had split up the 18 separate operations in this production process between 10 men, who each specialized in completing one or two operations. Using this method the firm produced 48,000 pins each day, an increase from 20 pins to 480 pins per man. Nowadays, many production processes are split up into their constituent operations, and workers are becoming more and more specialized. This has certain advantages and disadvantages, and these are listed below.

The advantages of the division of labour

1. Each man can do the job in which his superiority is most marked and for which he has the greatest aptitude.
2. Each man performs only a certain part of the production process and with practice can become highly dextrous at this operation, i.e. 'practice makes perfect'.
3. As fewer skills are required by each worker the time (and the cost) of training is reduced.
4. Workers do not have to switch from one operation to another, and thus time is saved.
5. Each worker will only need the tools to complete the operation which he performs and fewer tools are required. These tools will be used much more, and will not stand idle. The division of the production process into small parts also enables the use of specialized machinery.

The disadvantages of the division of labour

1. The major disadvantage of the division of labour is that the high degree of specialization and the continuous repetition of a single task is very monotonous. This may reduce a worker's motivation,

and it may also create poor industrial relations. It has been suggested that the basic cause of the high number of stoppages in car assembly plants is boredom, as workers will do anything to change their routine.

2. Loss of craftsmanship. The number of operations involved in some processes is so numerous that it is unlikely that a worker could alone produce a finished article and this invariably leads to a loss of craftsmanship. It should be noted, however, that the operation of some machines requires a high degree of skill.

3. The division of labour increases the risk of unemployment as a particular operation may put in a machine to replace a worker. Further, should an industry fall into decline a person who is highly specialized might find it difficult to find employment in other industries.

4. Interdependence. In a modern society everyone is dependent on everyone else. This is usually shown up during an industrial dispute in certain industries, where a strike by a handful of workers can lay off thousands of others.

Limits to the division of labour

The basic aim of the division of labour is to increase output. However, it is pointless to increase output if no-one wishes to purchase it. The demand for some goods is so small that there is little scope for the division of labour. In the case of the pin making factory there would be no point of specialization if only 20 pins could be sold each day.

Unemployment

In March 1982 almost three million unemployed persons were able and willing to work and were in search of a job. One of the major tasks of government since the end of the war has been to maintain full employment, that is, a situation where everyone who wants to work can do so.

The demand for the government to act in this way was created by the consistently high levels of unemployment in the inter-war years, when on average 14 per cent of the working population was unemployed. At certain times in some areas only one man in ten had a job. It was realized that there were two tragic problems associated with unemployment. Firstly, there was a loss in potential output to the nation which could never be obtained in the future, i.e. it was a loss for all time. Secondly, unemployment placed an enormous economic and psychological burden on those who were unemployed.

After 1945, levels of unemployment were far lower than they had been during the 1920s and the 1930s, and until 1965 between 1 per cent and 2 per cent of the working population was unemployed. From 1965 to 1972 the trend was upwards, and the beginning of 1972 saw a total of over one million. Despite a fall in unemployment during 1972 and 1973 unemployment began to increase again in the second half of 1973 and reached a peak of just under a million and a half in September 1977 (6·2 per cent of the working population). From September 1977 to December 1979 the rate fell slightly to about 1·3 million. However, during 1980 and 1981 there was a huge increase in unemployment – nearly 800,000 extra persons became unemployed in each of these years pushing the unemployment figure to 3·0 million (11% of the working population).

The main types of unemployment are as follows.

1. Frictional unemployment. A short period of unemployment is often involved when individuals change their job. This is not a serious problem as the frictionally unemployed soon return to work.

2. Seasonally unemployed. Some areas and occupations suffer from seasonal changes in employment. Seaside resorts often experience higher rates of unemployment during the winter months, and the bad weather sometimes forces building firms to lay off workers.

3. Structural unemployment. This is probably the most serious form of unemployment, as it can lead to high rates of unemployment in certain areas of the country, and the prospect of being unemployed for long periods for some people. Structural unemployment refers to the unemployment which occurs when major industries fall into decline, and are forced to lay off large numbers of workers. The reasons for the decline can be many, it may be due to intense foreign competition which makes the output of British firms commercially uneconomic, an example of this situation would be the production of textiles in the Far East which undermined the British textiles industry. Another reason might be a reduction in the demand for a product throughout the world because of innovation or technical developments. Shipyards throughout the world are having to lay off workers because of the large decline in the demand for ships. The former employees of declining industries may be unable to find work in their area, especially if the industry is highly localised (see Chapter 6), and even if they are geographically mobile they may be unable to find new employment without first undergoing a period of retraining.

4. Widespread deficiency of demand can cause general unemployment. The demand for labour depends to a large extent on the demand for goods and services. If, in general, firms experience a decline in demand for their output, they will lay off workers. This will cause unemployment in all industries, and must not be confused with structural unemployment, which may occur when the overall level of demand is high, and the rest of the industrial sector is doing well. The demand for firms' output is created by (a) spending by private individuals and firms in the U.K.; (b) spending by foreign individuals and firms on the output of British firms; (c) spending by the government.

Until 1979 all post-war governments had attempted to combat unemployment through their own spending. If private spending was considered to be too low the government increased its own spending, and reduced its spending when demand was high. This type of policy has not been used by the present Conservative government (1979–) for two reasons:

(i) the government believes that increased spending on its part would lead to a higher rate of inflation.

(ii) the government considers that the underlying cause of unemployment is structural and not demand deficient, and therefore that increasing demand would not be the appropriate policy for reducing unemployment.

There seems to be little doubt that demand management policies had been less effective in reducing unemployment during the 1970s than had been the case in the 1950s and 1960s.

Capital

In economics, capital does not simply mean money resources at our command. Capital normally refers to **capital goods** (also known as producer goods). Capital goods are those goods that man produces to help in the production of other goods. Primitive peoples make axes, simple spades and ploughs; in the advanced countries man builds nuclear power stations, blast furnaces and computerised assembly lines. All these are capital goods. Capital is therefore a man-made resource which is produced not for the satisfaction it gives to consumers, but for its ability to produce other goods. Capital is a comprehensive term and covers various types of capital.

Fixed capital consists of assets which have a comparatively long life, such as buildings and factories, fixed capital is used to produce other goods.

Circulating capital (also known as working capital) has a much shorter life and must be constantly replaced, it comprises commodities such as raw materials, which change their appearance in the productive process.

Social capital refers to capital which does not directly take part in production, such as houses, schools, roads, hospitals and libraries.

Capital accumulation

To increase its standard of living, a nation must increase its output of goods and services and this requires a growth in the nation's productive potential. Productive potential can be increased by accumulating capital. As output consists of consumer and capital goods and services, then if a nation wishes to accumulate capital goods, it must do so at the expense of consumer goods and services; i.e. to increase its future consumption a nation must first reduce present consumption and use more of its resources to produce capital. The production of new capital is called **investment.**

Capital consumption

During the productive process fixed capital is used up and the reduction in its value is referred to as capital consumption or depreciation. If worn-out capital is not replaced, a country's productive potential will fall, and this will almost certainly lead to a reduction in the standard of living.

The total amount of new investment is called **Gross investment,** whereas **Net investment** is the change in the stock of capital after capital consumption has been subtracted, thus

Gross investment – Capital consumption = Net investment

If net investment is negative then the stock of capital has fallen as capital consumption has exceeded gross investment; if net investment is positive, then the capital stock has increased.

The mobility of capital

Capital is geographically and occupationally mobile. A lorry, for example can be used in a variety of industries, and it can be transported from one location to another quite cheaply. Some capital goods are highly immobile in both senses. A large oil refinery is occupationally immobile, as it can only be used to produce petrochemicals – and it is most certainly geographically immobile.

Enterprise

Land, labour and capital do not produce anything by themselves. Some person must be prepared to organize them into a productive unit. This task of combining the factors of production to produce goods and services is performed by the entrepreneur, and is termed enterprise.

The role of the entrepreneur can be divided into two parts. Firstly, the entrepreneur takes the financial risk that the business involves, and can lose all the money he has put in the business if it fails. Secondly the entrepreneur is responsible for making the decisions about what is going to be produced, the location of production and the size of output. The entrepreneur considers these problems and decides the proportions of land, labour and capital to be used, knowing that payments have to be made in respect of rent for land or premises, wages for workers, interest charges on loan capital, before the goods reach the market, and before he knows whether or not people will buy the goods or services that the enterprise has produced.

In the past these two functions were carried out by one person as the large proportion of output was produced by small one-man businesses or partnerships. However, as firms have become larger and larger it has increasingly been the case that the two functions have been performed by different groups. The entrepreneurial function of organizing the factors of production is performed by skilled managers who receive a wage or salary and who are not entrepreneurs in the true sense as they do not take any financial risk. The risk-bearing function is today carried out by shareholders who invest in firms, but who take little or no part in management. This development has led many economists to the conclusion that enterprise is no longer a factor of production, since nowadays the classic function of the entrepreneur is performed by the factor of production, labour.

Key terms

Production refers to the process of fulfilling wants. Consumer goods are purchased by consumers for the satisfaction that they give.

Capital goods are produced because they help to produce other goods.

Services are mainly intangible things and are often produced and consumed at the same time.

Land, as a factor of production, is the term used to describe all natural resources available which are the gifts of nature.

Labour consists of the human resources which are available to take part in production.

Net investment is the addition to a nation's capital stock.

Capital consumption is the value of that capital which is used up in the productive process.

Chapter 3
The Scale of Production

In the early nineteenth century the majority of British firms were small one-man businesses and partnerships, and these firms produced the large part of the nation's output. Today, although the large proportion of firms remain quite small, it is the large firms which are now responsible for the lion's share of the nation's output, and the average size of the firm has increased considerably.

The major reason for this development is that as firms expand they often enjoy economies of scale. That is, as output expands costs increase less than proportionately, resulting in a lower cost per unit of output. A diseconomy of scale exists where costs increase more than proportionately as output expands. If a firm expands output from 100 units per week to 200 units per week, and the average cost of each unit falls from £1 to 70p, the firm is enjoying economies of scale. If the firm now increases output from 200 units per week to 300 units per week, and the average cost rises from 70p to 90p, the firm is experiencing diseconomies of scale.

The optimum size of output

A firm can be expected to produce at that level of output where the cost for each unit of output (also called average cost) is lowest, that is, it will continue to expand production until diseconomies of scale begin to exceed economies of scale. That level of output where average costs are lowest is called the optimum output. Optimum is a word which is used frequently in economics, and means 'best'.

Suppose a firm's costs behave as follows as output expands:

Output	Total cost (£)	Average cost (£)
1	100	100
2	180	90
3	240	80
4	280	70
5	300	60
6	450	75
7	630	90
8	880	110

These can be illustrated as in Figure 3.

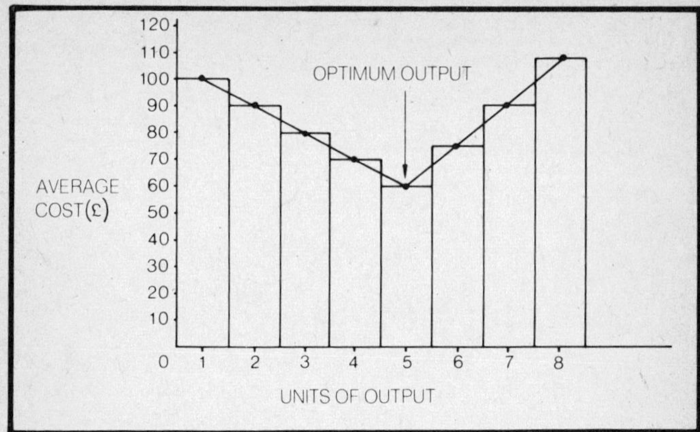

Figure 3. The optimum level of output

It can be seen, both from the table, and Figure 3, that the optimum output is 5 units, where the average cost is £60.
The economies of scale which reduce average costs, and the diseconomies which increase average costs are examined below.

Economies of scale

Economies of scale consist of (a) Internal economies and (b) external economies.

(a) Internal economies of scale

Internal economies of scale are those which a firm can obtain by increasing the scale of its operations, they can be classified as follows:

1. Technical economies

Technical aspects of many productive processes favour a large scale of production.

(i) Specialization By using the division of labour a firm can increase output considerably with only small increases in costs. Firms can also obtain large advantages by using specialised capital equipment.

(ii) Indivisibility of factors It is technically difficult to make certain factors of a particular size; some plants are only economically viable at a certain size. This may be too large for the small firm, and thus only large firms will enjoy the cost advantages of such processes. To some extent small firms can overcome this problem through combination.

(iii) Economies of increased dimensions If the length of each side of a cube is doubled, the volume of the cube is increased by eight times, whereas the surface area is only increased by four times. This physical fact means that firms can reduce their unit costs by increasing the dimensions of the vessels and containers they use, e.g. if the length, breadth and height of an oil tanker are doubled the volume of oil that can be carried is increased by eight times, but the quantity of steel required is only increased by four times.

(iv) The principle of multiples With the assembly line method of production the output of one machine is the input of another machine, and there may be several machines on one assembly line. Such machines often produce at different speeds, and large firms can compensate for this by having varying numbers of each machine. A small firm may only have one machine of each type and will therefore have men and machines idle for certain periods, with a loss in efficiency, and higher average costs.

2. Managerial economies

Large firms can apply the principle of the division of labour to management, hiring specialists in sales, marketing, production, finance, industrial relations, and so on. The small firm will have to rely on managers who try to fulfill all these functions and yet who may be specialist in none of them.

3. Commercial economies

Just as the housewife finds it cheaper to buy in large quantities, so does the firm. The large firm often pays less for raw materials and machinery because their suppliers are assured of large orders, and because they have a much stronger bargaining position than the smaller firms. Large firms can often afford to employ specialist buyers.

Large firms can also obtain advantages in selling, they can employ specialist sellers, use market research to conduct surveys, and may be able to afford to run advertising campaigns on the television and in the press. They can obtain cheaper rates for transporting their produce, or may operate their own transport system.

4. Financial economies

Most firms need to borrow money at some time or other to finance new investment, for example. The large firm will find it far easier to obtain loan capital, and it may be able to obtain such finance at a lower rate of interest than the smaller firm, as it will usually be considered to be more reliable than the small firm. The large firm will also be able to diversify its activities, so that if one part of its operation does badly it will be supported by the others. Small firms are unable to diversify in this way, and thus have a greater risk of bankruptcy.

(b) External economies of scale

External economies of scale are reductions in average costs which are the result of an increase in the size of the industry, or other factors which are external to the firm, e.g. better transport facilities. External economies provide advantages for all firms, both large and small, and are usually greater in industries where production is concentrated in a particular geographical area, and cost advantages accruing from localised production are called economies of concentration.

1. Economies of information, services and research

Groups of firms may circulate trade journals, and set up common research facilities. In some industries the government has aided the setting up of Research Associations, such as the British Ceramic Research Association. Of course, if a firm is large enough it may do all of these things itself.

2. Commercial economies

Ancillary services may become available to an industry, such as specialist banking and insurance services, haulage contractors who specialize in transporting the industry's output, firms which manufacture and service the machines and equipment used in the industry.

3. Labour

A skilled labour force, geared to working in certain industries is available in some areas of the country. Frequently, educational institutions provide courses to prepare people for the type of work performed in a local industry.

4. Disintegration

As an industry becomes larger, firms can specialize in certain aspects of production. In car assembly, for example, Lucas specialize in the production of electrical components.

Diseconomies of scale

These consist of (a) Internal diseconomies of scale and (b) External economies of scale.

(a) Internal diseconomies of scale

As firms increase in size the task of organising production becomes more and more difficult.

Organizations are often so large that communications between management and workers, and within management, are often strained. Communication is important as the quality of information that decision makers receive determines the quality of decision-making. Decision-making is often slow, as all the specialist management departments have to first be consulted. Even when a decision has been made, and assuming that communications are adequate, many large firms are so large that management may be unable to ensure that their decisions are carried out.

Large firms also find that the motivation of its employees is difficult, and workers often feel alienated from the firm. Poor management-worker relations, strikes and other forms of industrial dispute are far more common in large firms than in small ones.

(b) External diseconomies of scale

There are two major external diseconomies of scale. Firstly, if the industry grows very quickly, or becomes too large, supplies of resources used by the industry may become short in supply, and firms will tend to compete with each other to try to ensure that they have adequate supplies, and this may well increase firms' costs. For example, a shortage of skilled labour will encourage firms to offer higher wages to attract workers from other firms.
Secondly, diseconomies of concentration result if an industry becomes too concentrated in an area. Roads may become congested, leading to higher transport costs; workers will be less willing to work in the industry if this concentration has forced up the prices of houses, and resulted in an overcrowded polluted town. There is also the danger that if the industry declines the whole area may become depressed.

The growth of the firm

Private enterprise organizations produce goods and services to make the maximum profit possible. So it would seem reasonable to assume that the average size of the firm has increased because firms are thus able to achieve higher profits. Firms can grow in size in two ways, either by internal growth or through integration with other firms.

1. Internal growth

Internal growth is often obtained by using economies of scale so that production is at the optimum level of output. Firms growing through internal means often widen their range of products, whilst remaining in the same broad area of production. Dunlop tyres grew in this manner, expanding both their output of goods, and entering fields of production related to tyre production through the raw material, rubber, such as sports shoes and tennis balls. They then expanded into the production of other sports goods, not necessarily related to rubber.

2. Integration

Integration refers to the joining of two firms, and may take the form of a take-over or a merger. There are several motives for these mergers but a main one is the desire for greater profit. This higher profit may be the result of one of the following factors:

1. A greater share of the market.
2. Greater monopoly power over suppliers and buyers.
3. Rationalization of production through a reduction of duplicated work, and the reduction of labour forces.
4. A better integrated research programme.
5. A more diversified range of products.
6. The sale, or better use of the assets of one of the firms.
7. Access to new markets at home and abroad.
8. Greater availability of the economies of scale.

If the merger is successful, the new firm will be able to reduce its average costs, cut out waste and expand its markets. Good management skills will be vital to ensure the merger is successful for there have been several cases where newly merged firms have found themselves suffering from diseconomies of scale, on account of management difficulties in running the new firm.

There are three types of integration, (i) horizontal integration, (ii) vertical integration and (iii) conglomorate integration.

(i) Horizontal integration occurs when a firm expands its existing activities, by combining with a firm which operates at the same stage of production. A merger of two food retailing shops would be a horizontal merger. There have been several important mergers of this type, notably in the brewing industry, the car assembly industry, the tyre industry and banking.

(ii) Vertical integration occurs when two firms merge which produce at different stages in the production of the same good or service. If the dominant firm in the merger is gaining control of one of its suppliers it is called backward integration. If the dominant firm is gaining control of one of its customers it is called forward integration. Backward integration may be prompted by the desire to secure an adequate level of supplies, especially in periods of scarcity or high demand. Forward integration may be undertaken when the demand for the firm's output is uncertain and the producer wishes to obtain guaranteed market outlets.

(iii) Conglomorate integration occurs when two firms combine whose output is unrelated, or only slightly related. This type of merger is often pursued to enable firms to diversify their output so that if one of its products does badly its other products can be expected to ensure a reasonable return, and thus the firm will not fail. Sometimes, these mergers can bring management and marketing benefits.

The small firm

For statistical purposes the small firm is defined as an enterprise with less than 200 employees. Despite the various factors which encourage the average size of the firm to increase there are over one million small firms in operation in Britain today. The Bolton Committee on Small Firms (1971) identified two functions of small firms which were of crucial importance—'as a breeding ground of new industries and the source of dynamic competition'. On the recommendation of the Bolton Committee the Department of Industry set up a separate division which is the focal point for the formation of government policy towards small firms. The division also administers a chain of small firms centres throughout Great Britain which provide an information and counselling service for small businessmen.

In 1981 several measures were announced which are designed to help the small business. These include a bank loan guarantee scheme under which the Government guarantees 80 per cent of bank loans approved by the Department of Industry, and a business start-up scheme under which tax concessions are made to private individuals investing in small businesses. Furthermore, small companies pay a reduced rate of Corporation tax (40 per cent instead of the normal 52 per cent).

The major reasons for the continued existence of the small firm can be identified as:

1. Personal service

Small firms are able to provide a personal service to their customers. Small retail shops may charge higher prices, but shoppers are sometimes prepared to accept these for the personal service that they would not receive if they shopped in a supermarket.

2. Individuality versus standardization

Many small firms produce individualistic goods, which appeal to that part of the community who prefer to purchase nonstandardized produce. A man may prefer to buy his clothes from a bespoke tailor so that he can wear clothes of a different style to those available in most clothes shops.

3. Transport costs

If transport costs are too high, firms may be unable to deliver beyond a certain distance, this will limit the size of the firm. On the other hand, high transport costs will deter people from travelling too far and this will favour the small local shop at the expense of the shops in city centres and the out-of-town hypermarkets.

4. Luxury goods

Some goods have a small market because they are so expensive that few people can afford to buy them. Firms producing such items will therefore tend to remain small.

5. Disintegration

If an industry is subject to disintegration, a firm may remain small because it produces a large quantity of units, which supply the whole industry, and yet which have little value.

6. Co-operation

Small firms can sometimes reduce their costs by co-operation. They may buy supplies in bulk, share expensive capital equipment, advertise and even establish a joint research department.

7. Business motives

Small firms will continue to exist whilst some people have a desire to have their own business, and to work for themselves.

Key terms

The optimum size of output is that level where average costs are lowest.

Internal economies of scale are those factors which reduce average costs as the scale of production increases.

Internal diseconomies are those factors which increase average costs as production increases.

External economies (diseconomies) of scale are those reductions (increases) in average costs which are the result of an increase in the size of the industry.

Integration refers to the joining of two firms.

Chapter 4
The Costs of Production

A firm engaged in production will incur various costs which will have to be paid if it is to continue in business. A firm will also need to know the level of costs connected with a particular level of output, so that it can determine that level of output at which its costs per unit will be lowest, i.e. the optimum level of output. Costs are classified under the following headings:

1. Fixed costs (FC) do not vary with output. They are sometimes referred to as overhead costs or supplementary costs. The main components of fixed costs are (a) *rent and rates,* (b) *depreciation,* (c) *interest and loans.* These are all fixed costs as if the firm produced nothing at all, or thousands of units of output these costs would remain the same. Other fixed costs include some types of labour costs, such as night-watchmen and possibly maintenance men. However, fixed costs are only fixed for a given time. In the long run all costs are variable, for example, in the long run, if the firm produces large quantities it will probably require larger premises, which will involve higher rent and rates. Furthermore, a larger output might also necessitate a greater quantity of plant and machinery, and thus depreciation will rise.

2. Variable costs (VC) are sometimes called prime costs, and are those expenses which vary with output. The main variable costs are labour, power and raw materials. The higher the output of the firm, the greater will be its variable costs. Variable costs do not rise at a uniform rate as they are subject to economies and diseconomies of scale. That is, variable costs can be expected to rise less than proportionately up to a point as the firm enjoys the advantages of scale economies, but once the optimum level of output has been passed variable costs rise more than proportionately.

It is sometimes difficult to determine whether a particular cost is fixed or variable. However if the cost rises as output expands, it is a variable cost.

3. Total cost (TC) is the addition of fixed and variable costs. Total costs always increase with an expanding output.
The following example shows the cost schedules and curves of a small firm producing wooden tables.

Units of output	Fixed cost (£)	Variable cost (£)	Total cost (£)
0	150	—	150
1	150	50	200
2	150	90	240
3	150	120	270
4	150	150	300
5	150	200	350
6	150	270	420
7	150	361	511
8	150	474	624
9	150	615	765
10	150	800	950

Table 2. Fixed costs, variable costs and total costs.

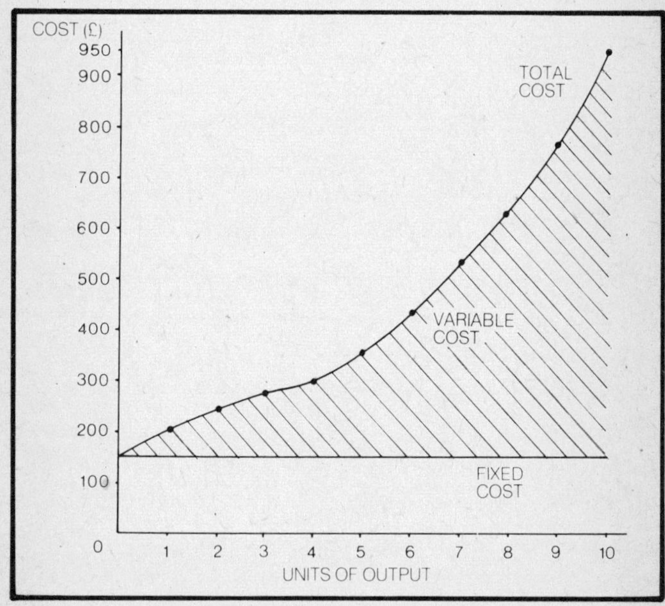

Figure 4. Total cost curve, fixed cost curve, and variable cost

4. Average cost (AC) is also known as cost per unit, and is obtained by dividing total costs by units of output. Average cost tends to be high at first, due to the fixed cost element, and then falls, but begins to rise again after a point. Average cost is important to the entrepreneur, as it gives the lowest possible unit cost, which is also the optimum output, beyond which diminishing returns set in. The total and average cost schedules for the production of wooden tables is given below.

Units of output	Total cost (£)	Average cost (£)
0	150	—
1	200	200
2	240	120
3	270	90
4	300	75
5	350	70
6	420	70
7	511	73
8	624	78
9	765	85
10	950	95

Table 3. Total cost and average cost schedules.

It should be noted immediately that there are two levels of output where average costs are at a minimum. If the firm produces five or six tables average costs are £70.

Units of output	Total cost (£)	Marginal cost (£)
0	150	—
1	200	50
2	240	40
3	270	30
4	300	30
5	350	50
6	420	70
7	511	91
8	624	113
9	765	141
10	950	185

Table 4. Total cost and marginal cost schedules.

5. Marginal cost (MC) is also of great importance to the entrepreneur. Marginal means 'extra', and thus the marginal cost of a unit of output is the extra cost (i.e. the change in total cost) that has resulted from the production of one extra unit. The total and marginal cost schedules for the output of wooden tables is shown on the preceding page.

A marginal cost curve and an average cost curve can be drawn on the basis of the marginal and average cost schedules, and these curves are illustrated in Figure 5.

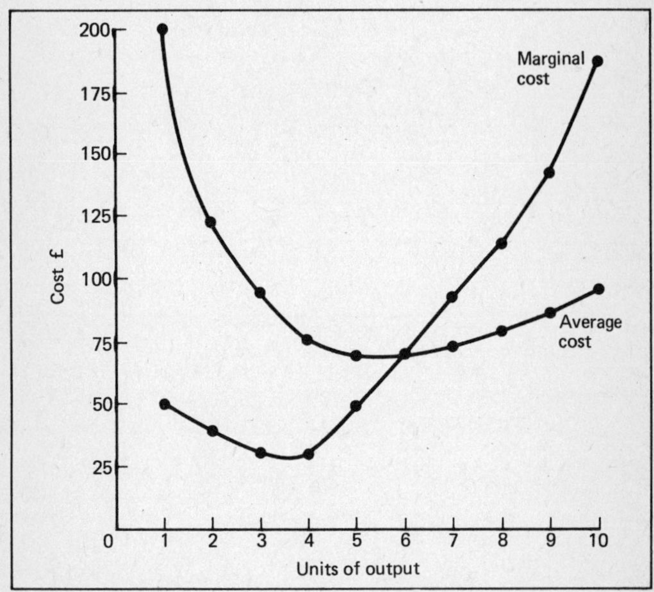

Figure 5. The marginal cost curve and the average cost curve

There are three important facts which are shown by Figure 5.
1. When marginal cost is below (less than) average cost, average cost is falling.
2. When marginal cost is above (greater than) average cost, average cost is rising.
3. Average cost and marginal cost are equal at the lowest point on the average cost curve, i.e. AC = MC at the optimum output.

6. Normal profit It may seem strange to include a 'profit' under the heading 'costs', but normal profit is a cost of the firm which must be paid to ensure the firm continues in the same line of business.

The concept of normal profit creates problems for some students. Profit is normally understood to be that figure obtained by deducting costs of production from the sales revenue. However, the entrepreneur who has financed the firm, and who is risking his money will have a clear idea of the sort of return he wants if he is to continue to keep his money in the firm. This can be considered to be a minimum return which will keep him in the existing line of production. After all, he could put money in a building society, or some other institution where he can earn interest without taking any risks. The rate of return which is just sufficient to keep him in his present line of business is known as normal profit. Normal profit is a cost of the business as if it is not earned by the entrepreneur, then in the long run the firm will stop production. In fact, normal profit is the opportunity cost of the finance provided by the entrepreneur.
Normal profit will be included in the costs of production, and therefore when the average cost of a certain level of output is equal to the average revenue that is obtained from selling this output, the firm is not just breaking even, it is earning normal profits.

Key terms

Fixed costs are those expenses which do not vary with output.
Variable costs are those expenses which vary with output.
Total cost is the sum of fixed costs and variable costs.
Average cost is the cost per unit of output, and is obtained by dividing total cost by units of output.
Marginal cost is the change in total cost resulting from the production of an extra unit of output.
Normal profit is the opportunity cost of the finance provided by an entrepreneur for a firm.

Chapter 5
Business Organization

There are almost 3 million business organizations in the United Kingdom, ranging from the small one-man business to the giant private organizations such as Unilever and British Petroleum, and the nationalized industries like the Post Office and the National Coal Board.

Business organizations are classified under three main headings, dependent upon their ownership and organization, these are:

A. Private enterprise
B. Cooperative enterprise
C. Public enterprise

A. Private enterprise

Private enterprise organization can be sub-divided into the one-man business, the partnership and the joint-stock company.

1. The one-man business

The one-man business or sole-proprietor describes a firm owned and invariably run by a single person. This type of business is usually financed from a person's savings, and by borrowing from friends, relatives, banks and finance companies. The major advantages of the one-man business are that the owner retains personal control and receives personal rewards for initiative and effort. The main disadvantages are firstly, that the owner may have limited resources and may find borrowing difficult. Secondly, the one-man business does not enjoy the benefits of limited liability (see joint-stock companies, below). Thirdly, as the success of this type of business is determined by one person, they tend to suffer from a lack of continuity, for when the original owner wishes to leave the business there may not be another person who is able to take over the business.

One-man businesses tend to be most numerous in those sectors of industry where personal service is important. Examples are services such as shoe-repairing, hairdressing and retailing.

2. The partnership

A partnership is a voluntary combination of between two and twenty persons who jointly provide the firm's capital and share the profits.

The main advantages of the partnership are that more capital is available than with the one-man business, furthermore partners can specialize in certain areas of the business. Decision making is reasonably flexible and personal rewards for initiative and effort can be made.

The main disadvantages are that a lack of capital may still hinder a firm's growth, and should disagreements occur between partners management of the firm may prove to be difficult. Probably the greatest disadvantage is that partnerships do not, on the whole, enjoy limited liability and thus partners are financially responsible for the actions of each other.

Some firms have 'sleeping partners', who provide capital, but do not work and may have little say in the running of the firm, accordingly they usually receive a smaller share of the profits. 'Active partners' in some circumstances will not contribute capital to the firm and their income will be related to the firm's profits rather than to the hours they work.

The Limited Partnership Act of 1907 enables a person to become a 'limited' partner so that if the firm goes bankrupt he only stands to lose the money he has invested in the firm.

Partnerships are most commonly found in sectors of industry where the capital requirement is low, and where partners have the opportunity to specialize, such as the professions (law, accountancy), estate agents and retailing.

3. The joint-stock company

The joint-stock company is a firm where the capital is raised by the sale of shares to the public and where any profits are distributed to the holders of shares. Companies are a legal entity, distinct from the shareholders who own the company, and can take legal action, own property, enter into contracts and be sued; furthermore the life span of its shareholders does not determine the life span of the company, and this ensures the continuity of the firm. Shareholders of companies enjoy limited liability, introduced by the 1862 *Limited Liability Act*; this means an investor's liabilities are limited to his investment. The 1862 Act was a major factor in encouraging the formation of joint-stock companies. Prior to that time even the smallest shareholder could lose all his possessions if the firm failed and this proved a great deterrent to the formation of companies. Following abuses of the joint-stock system in the eighteenth century the government introduced legislation designed to protect shareholders from fraudulent activities carried out by those persons forming the company. Nowadays the Registrar of Companies has to approve 'The Memorandum of

Association' and 'The Articles of Association', which give details concerning the company, such as its internal organization, its objectives and its nominal capital. The company may start business once the Registrar has given his approval and issued The Certificate of Trading.
There are two types of joint-stock company, (a) the private company and (b) the public company. The legal and financial obligations of the two are rather different and therefore they are examined separately.

(a) Private companies

Private companies must have a minimum of 2 shareholders, but have a maximum number of 50. They must, by law, sell their shares privately and cannot offer them for sale to the public. Furthermore no shareholder can sell his shares without the consent of the board of directors.

The main advantages of the private company are:

1. The shareholders enjoy limited liability.
2. The firm is able to obtain more capital than the partnership and the one-man business.
3. The firm is unlikely to have the problems associated with continuity.

The main disadvantages of the private company are:

1. The firm may have to pay higher rates of tax as companies are liable for corporation tax, once they have reached a particular size.
2. The firm may still have insufficient funds to expand as it has a maximum of 50 shareholders.

Private companies obtain their finance from three main sources:
(a) selling their shares
(b) by ploughing back profits
(c) by borrowing from a merchant bank or some other specialist lender such as Finance For Industry (FFI) – these institutions are examined later in this chapter.

In 1981, there were almost 700,000 registered private companies in Britain, although it is estimated that some 300,000 of them are dormant. Although private companies are more numerous than public companies, private companies are much smaller on average, and their contribution to total output is quite small.
Many private companies are family firms, which have sought the advantages of limited liability and extra capital, whilst the family has sought to retain control.

(b) Public companies

In 1981 there were almost 17,000 public companies, although 13,500 were inactive. A public company must have a minimum of 7 shareholders but there is no maximum number; further, at least two persons must be named as directors. Unlike private companies shares can be offered for sale to the public, who may then re-sell the shares as frequently as they desire, i.e. the board of directors does not have to give permission before shares can be sold.

The main advantages of the public company are:

1. Limited liability.
2. The free transferability of shares and the ability of companies to sell shares to the public means that large amounts of capital can be obtained, and thus a lack of capital should not prevent expansion.
3. As the firm is large it can employ specialists in many fields and thus does not suffer from the problems which accompany a lack of continuity.
4. Individuals can invest small amounts in companies without having to take an active part in management.

The main disadvantages of the public company are:

1. Corporation tax has to be paid.
2. The large number of shares and shareholders means that a divorce between ownership and control may follow, i.e. those who collectively own the company are so numerous and so diverse that it is management that effectively controls the firm, and in doing so may follow objectives other than the objectives of the owners.

Company finance

Public companies obtain their finance from four main sources.

1. Retained profits

Firms can either distribute profits to their shareholders or retain them for investment purposes. Certain tax advantages accrue to firms which reinvest earnings rather than distribute them to shareholders. Almost 70% of investment by public companies is financed from retained profits.

2. Shares

On becoming a public company a firm can obtain large amounts of new capital by selling shares. In fact many private companies have 'gone public' so as to obtain funds for expansion. Existing public companies tend not to issue new shares to finance investment, but use one of the other methods specified.

There are two main types of shares, preference shares and ordinary shares (also called 'equity').

Preference shares entitle the holder to a fixed return from the company's profits. If the company has a good year and profits are high the preference shareholder will receive his entitlement and no more, whereas if the company makes a loss he will receive nothing. However, the preference shareholder has the right to be paid before any other shareholders, and thus in a poor year the preference shareholder may well receive payment whilst the other shareholders receive nothing. As little risk accompanies preference shares they rarely entitle the holder to any say in the running of the company. The return on a share financed from a company's profits is called a dividend.

Ordinary shares receive a dividend, the size of which depends on the profitability of the company. If the company fares badly and makes a loss or a very small profit the ordinary shareholders will receive nothing. If the company does well the ordinary share will earn a high dividend. The ordinary share therefore carries the greatest risk and thus the power to vote on the running of the company.

When public companies wish to raise additional finance to pay for expansion, they may attempt to do so by an issue of new shares. However, new shares are not sold on the Stock Exchange (a popular misconception), as only second-hand shares are transacted here. The Stock Exchange does, however, influence the amount of new investment available to firms. If a second-hand market did not exist investors would be unwilling to buy shares as they would be unable to sell them when they wished to do so; it is in this way that the Stock Exchange aids the raising of new capital.

3. Debentures

A debenture is a loan to a firm with a fixed rate of interest and normally a redemption date, on which the loan will be repaid. The holders of debentures are creditors of the firm and as such receive payment before preference shareholders and ordinary shareholders. A £100 6% debenture for 20 years issued in 1980 will guarantee the investor £6 every year until 2000 when the £100 loan will be repaid. In times of high inflation and high interest rates this type of financing is unpopular with firms because they have to offer high interest rates with the possibility that if interest rates fall they will have an expensive loan on their hands. In the past loans have accounted for 10% of investment by firms.

4. Bank borrowing

For their short-term needs companies borrow money from the banks, although it is not uncommon for this short-term borrowing to become long-term borrowing. Bank borrowing accounts for about 10% of company finance.

Specialist sources of finance

There exist three major financial institutions which specialize in providing finance to private and public companies.

Finance for Industry (FFI) was set up in 1973 and has two major subsidiaries. The Industrial and Commercial Finance Corporation (ICFC) was established in 1945 by the clearing banks and the Bank of England; it provides medium and long-term funds at fixed interest rates for small and medium sized firms. At the end of March 1981 it had gross facilities outstanding of £451 million in 3,900 companies. The Finance Corporation for Industry (FCI) is the second main subsidiary of FFI; it provides medium term finance for larger firms and during the year ended March 1981 advanced a total of £45 million.

Equity Capital for Industry (ECI) was set up in 1976, with a capital of £42 million to supply long-term finance in the form of equity to British firms.

The British Technology Group (BTG) is a public corporation formed by the merger of the National Research Development Corporation (NRDC) and the National Enterprise Board (NEB). The NRDC was set up in 1949 to promote the development and the exploitation of new technology. The NRDC has some 700 investments in development projects of which about 680 are joint ventures with industrial companies. The NEB was created by the 1975 Industry Act to hold shareholdings previously held by the government in BL, Rolls Royce and Ferranti. It was issued with new guidelines in 1980 giving it an investment role in firms developing advanced technologies and in the English Assisted Areas; it also grants loans of up to £50,000 to small firms. The NEB is required to dispose of its shareholdings to private ownership as soon as it is commercially practicable.

B. Cooperative enterprise

A cooperative enterprise is a type of business organization where the plant, equipment and stocks of goods are owned collectively by those with a direct interest in the articles sold or services provided. Both producers' and consumers' cooperatives exist.

Producers' cooperatives

A producers' cooperative exists where the ownership and control of an enterprise rests with those who work in it. There are only a few producers' cooperatives in Britain, mostly in printing, textiles, footwear production and agriculture. Probably the most widely known producers' cooperative is the department store group, The John Lewis Partnership.

Consumers' cooperatives

A consumers' cooperative is an enterprise where the ownership and control of the enterprise rests with the consumers of the firm's output. Consumers' cooperatives have been quite popular in Britain since the first retailing cooperative was set up in Rochdale in 1844. The original idea of the 24 weavers who began it was to sell groceries in their own retail store to members and share out the profits according to the value of each member's purchases. Retail cooperative societies began to spring up throughout the country. In 1873 the retail cooperatives combined to form the **Cooperative Wholesale Society** (CWS) as some existing wholesalers refused to supply them, and they realised that in combination they would be able to demand lower prices from manufacturers. Membership of the CWS is restricted to retail cooperatives, among whom any profits are distributed. Over the years the CWS has expanded its activities and now owns factories and farms. In 1980 the CWS had a turnover of £1,807 million and supplied about two-thirds of the requirements of the retail societies.

Increased competition in the retail trade has favoured larger organizations and has led to a large number of amalgamations of retail societies. In 1958 there were 1,000 societies but by 1980 this number had fallen to 187. In 1980 the retail cooperative societies had total sales of £3,950 million (6·4% of total retail trade) and had 9·9 million members. Nowadays the profits are shared out to members by the use of trading stamps. During the year members receive stamps with their purchases and the society's level of profit will determine the value of each stamp and thus each member's dividend.

The major advantage of the cooperative is that the enterprise and its profits belong to the producers and consumers and not to some remote shareholders or the state. This means that members are more likely to support the concern and will favour the reinvestment of profit.

The major disadvantage is that cooperation may be inspired by ideological motives, and this may not be a good basis for business success. Secondly, producers' cooperatives often require a larger input of capital than can be obtained by the combination of a number of workers, and thus cooperation is very difficult in some cases.

C. Public enterprise

In the United Kingdom the state enters into commercial activities through the nationalized industries, which in 1980 produced 11%

of the nation's output, employed 8 % of Britain's labour force (1·7 million) and accounted for 20 % of the U.K.'s gross investment in plant and equipment. The National Economic Development Office (NEDO) has defined nationalized industries as those public corporations whose boards of directors are appointed by the government, but who are not civil servants and are primarily engaged in industrial or other trading activities. In this definition there are eleven major nationalized industries – the National Coal Board, British Gas, the electricity industry and the British National Oil Corporation; the British Steel Corporation and British Shipbuilders; the Post Office and British Telecommunications; British Rail, the National Bus Company and British Airways. Other public corporations which do not qualify as being nationalized industries on the strict NEDO definition include the Regional Water Authorities, Port Authorities, The Bank of England and the British Technology Group (which has substantial holding in BL). The majority of the publicly owned industries were created by the first post-war Labour government of 1945–1951, although it would be wrong to suggest that public enterprise is purely a post-war phenomenon. As early as the 1860s the Post Office had taken over the private telegraph companies; it had been the municipal authorities and borough councils which had organized local supplies of gas and electricity during the second half of the nineteenth century. Other pre-war nationalization included the British Overseas Airways Corporation (which was combined with British European Airways in 1971 to form British Airways), the British Broadcasting Corporation, the London Transport Board and the Port of London. Furthermore, the nationalization of the coal mining industry, which occurred in 1947 had been recommended as early as 1919 by the Sankey commission.

Although the Conservatives denationalized the steel industry in 1953, it was renationalized in 1967. In 1968 the National Bus Company was formed to take responsibility for certain government holdings in passenger road transport, and the National Freight Corporation took over government holdings in road haulage, some of which had been previously owned by British Rail. In 1969 the Post Office was changed from a government ministry into a nationalized industry and in 1977 the Labour government of 1974–1979 nationalized the aerospace industry to form British Aerospace and also the shipbuilding and shiprepairing industry to form British Shipbuilders, although various governments had been deeply involved in this industry for years. The Conservative government (1979–) has made some important changes to the size and structure of the nationalized industries. In 1980 the National Freight Corporation and British Aerospace were changed into limited companies with shares owned by the Government as a first step in their transfer to private ownership. In 1981 the telecommunications division of the Post Office became a separate entity – British Telecom.

The extent of public enterprise in Britain is not too different to that in other European countries, as is shown in the table below.

Country	Public enterprise employment
Austria	13·7
Belgium	5·2
Britain	8·1
France	7·3
West Germany	7·2
Holland	3·6
Ireland	7·3
Italy	6·6
Sweden	8·2

Table 5. Employment in public enterprises as a percentage of the labour force.

The European industries commonly found under public enterprise include the posts, telecommunications, electricity, gas, coal, railways and the airlines. Several nations have also nationalized the shipbuilding, steel and motor vehicle manufacturing industries.

It is important to examine the reasons for nationalization together with the economic arguments for and against this form of enterprise.

Reasons for public enterprise

The publicly owned industries in the United Kingdom were nationalized for one or more of the following reasons:

1. To control monopoly power

(a) Natural monopolies. An important reason for nationalization is that some industries are 'natural' monopolies, and under private enterprise competing companies might duplicate the provision of services. For example, two or more water, gas, electricity or telephone companies might provide their connections to a single street and attempt to persuade consumers to buy their output. It is likely that a monopoly would soon form, giving customers no choice of supply, and providing the firm with considerable power over the consumer. This was the case with the early public utilities and railways. Nationalization ensures that wasteful duplication is avoided and that the natural monopolies are used in the interests of the whole community.

(b) Economies of scale. Some productive processes are subject to economies of scale that are so large that monopoly or monopolistic competition would result if left in private hands. In this case nationalization can ensure that the industry operates at its most efficient level of output, and prevents the abuse of the power of monopoly.

2. To provide capital

Private industry may be unwilling or unable to provide the capital investment needed for infant industries. Atomic energy is a case in point, although other reasons are important here too. Some existing industries suffer from a similar problem when requiring large capital investments to finance big technological changes. For example, the NCB will require investment of £500 million per year if it is to meet its target output of 170 million tons per year by the year 2000.

3. To manage the contraction of a declining industry

This was the reason for the nationalization of shipbuilding and to some extent the public ownership of the steel and coal industries. In private hands such industries decline so quickly that social problems of great magnitude occur.

4. To cover the divergence between private and social costs and benefits. In this case a nationalized industry can, via the tax-payer, provide a service which may be commercially uneconomic yet socially profitable. In 1980 British Rail received government subsidies of some £634 million to run uneconomic railway services.

5. Security of supplies

Nationalization may be needed to ensure the operation of a strategic industry essential to the national security or independence. Examples include shipbuilding, coal and atomic energy.

6. National planning

Public ownership of basic industries makes possible the planning of national policy to prevent the waste of resources and unnecessary competition. This is the case with fuel industries, and although coal, gas and electricity compete vigorously, the government plans that coal and nuclear energy will replace oil and gas when these run out.

Arguments against public enterprise

1. Diseconomies of scale

It is argued that some nationalized industries experience diseconomies of scale because they are too large. Their size makes them difficult to manage requiring large bureaucracies which are inevitably inefficient, and have a poor quality output. It is claimed that this problem has been worsened by the inadequate rewards for nationalized industry management which failed to attract good managers and resulted in poor quality management.

2. Insufficient competition

Many people believe that competition encourages efficiency, and that the lack of competition experienced by the nationalized industries, due to their monopoly position has resulted in sloppy management, and a lack of determination to reduce costs and use resources efficiently. This does not apply to the extent which critics claim, and the degree of competition varies greatly. The gas, coal and electricity industries compete with each other as a source of energy. British Rail (which accounts for about 8% of passenger travel) has to compete with other forms of transport – buses and private cars. British Airways has a great deal of competition on some routes, both from the state airlines of other countries and private airlines. The British Steel Corporation and British Shipbuilders face intense foreign competition – often from the public enterprises of other nations.

3. Misuse of monopoly power

A reason for placing an industry under public control is to ensure that monopoly power is used in the interests of the community as a whole. There have been charges levelled at the nationalized industries that they have abused their monopoly position by charging high prices for their output. The 1980 Competition Act enables the Secretary of State to refer to the Monopolies and Mergers Commission any question on the possible abuse of a monopoly situation by bodies in the public sector.

4. Political interference

The British nationalized industries have suffered considerably from political interference by all governments. During the 1950s they were given conflicting objectives in that they were instructed to provide an adequate service, to break even and to be efficient. Too frequently, nationalized industries have been forced to neglect long-term investment plans to obtain short-term advantages for one government or another. It is argued that the ability and willingness of governments to meddle in this way provides a sound argument against public enterprise.

Control of public corporations

Public corporations are established by Act of Parliament, and are given certain functions, usually expressed in terms of providing certain goods and services for the public, in the respective nationalization Act. Public corporations are publicly owned and their assets are vested in the corporation board, which in some ways can be compared to the board of directors in a joint stock company. The public corporation is a legal entity and has the power to employ labour, enter into contracts, own assets, sue and be sued, and so on.

Public control over the public corporation is achieved in three ways by:

1. Ministerial control. The appropriate Minister is given certain powers under the nationalization Act, and his role can in some ways be compared to that of the shareholder in the joint stock company.

Firstly, the Minister appoints (and can dismiss) the chairman and members of the board. Secondly, the Minister gives general policy directions, although he is not expected to interfere in the day-to-day running of the corporation. Thirdly, the Minister approves the general programme of capital development and research. Fourthly, the Minister is usually empowered to decide what shall be done with any surplus revenues.

2. Parliamentary control. The House of Commons Select Committee on the Nationalized Industries examines the reports and accounts of the corporations and has the power to send for persons, papers and records.

3. Consumers' Consultative or Advisory Councils. Nationalization Acts generally require the Minister responsible to see that the interests of the industry's consumers are safeguarded, and this is usually done by setting up Consultative or Advisory Councils which consider complaints and suggestions, and may make recommendations to the board and to the Minister.

Organization of public corporations

The internal organization of the public corporations varies considerably. The Coal Industry Nationalization Act of 1946 set up a National Board which was given the task of determining an internal organization which would best enable it to perform its statutory duties. However, when the gas and electricity industries were nationalized, Area boards were made responsible for the distribution of electricity and the supply of gas, each board was free to determine its own organizational structure. Discovery of North Sea gas created the need for a centralized organization to administer the distribution of gas, and in 1973 the British Gas Corporation was formed to perform this task, thereby centralizing control of the industry.

In general the public corporations are given an internal organization which will best suit its own needs – whatever these might be.

Financial obligations

The financial obligations of nationalized industries, and the principles upon which they should operate are laid down in Government White Papers. They are required to balance their books 'taking one year with another', and they are required to set their prices on the basis of marginal costs.

In effect the commercial operation of all the nationalized industries is often restricted by their statutes, and by the intervention of the Minister.

Key terms

The one-man business is a firm owned and invariably run by a single person.

The partnership is a voluntary combination of between two and twenty persons who jointly provide the firm's capital and share the profits.

A private joint stock company can have between 2 and 50 shareholders, but may not appeal to the public to buy shares.

A public joint stock company raises capital by offering shares to the public. There must be at least 7 shareholders, but there is no upper limit.

A debenture is a loan to a firm with a fixed rate of interest and normally a redemption date.

In a **cooperative enterprise,** the plant, equipment and stocks of goods are owned collectively. In a consumers' cooperative they are owned by the consumers of the firm's output. In a producers' cooperative they are owned by those who work in it.

Public enterprise refers to the entry of the state into commercial activities. In the U.K. this is done through the nationalized industries.

Nationalized industries (according to the strict definition of the National Economic Development Office), are those public corporations whose boards of directors are appointed by the government, but who are not civil servants, and which are primarily engaged in industrial or other trading activities.

Chapter 6
Distribution

The Distributive trade provides the connecting link between producers and consumers. There are two main sectors within the distributive trades, wholesaling and retailing, and together they employed over two and a half million people in 1980 (approximately 10% of the working population). Retailers and wholesalers provide a valuable service in assuring that goods are available to the consumer when, where, and in the quantities that they are required.

The distributive process

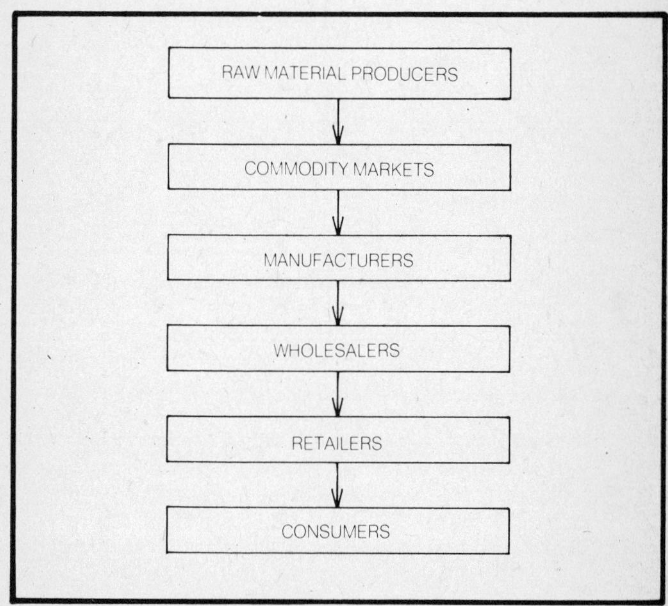

Figure 6. The distributive process

A simple example showing the basic distributive process is shown in Figure 6. The sections of this process which are considered to be part of the distributive trade are:

(A) The commodity markets.
(B) Wholesalers
(C) Retailers

(A) The commodity markets

The link between the extractors of raw materials and the manufacturers who use these raw materials to produce other goods is provided by the commodity markets. Several of the world's commodity markets are in London, although the business transacted is international, and the produce traded is sent from the country of extraction to the buying nation direct, without passing through London. Important examples of the London commodity markets are The London Wool Exchange, and The London Metal Exchange for lead, tin, copper and zinc.

Commodities are traded using two methods: auctions, and private agreements between dealers. The second method has given rise to 'futures' trading. A buyer guards against a possible rise in price by contracting now the price he will pay for his future requirements of a commodity, and a seller guards against a fall in price by selling in advance future quantities of the item. These speculative activities tend to keep the price of a product stable.

(B) Wholesaling

The distinguishing characteristic of wholesaling is that the wholesaler operates between business units. The majority of wholesalers act as a link between manufacturers and retailers, although others operate in the commodity markets trading in raw materials. Traditionally, wholesalers have specialized in one product area. Their main trading areas being (a) food, (b) clothing and textiles, (c) electrical and hardware, (d) industrial materials, (e) coal, builders supplies and agricultural supplies. In recent years the degree of specialization has fallen as wholesalers have sought ways to retain profit levels in the face of competition from manufacturers and retailers.

Distribution methods vary considerably in different product areas. Fruit and vegetables, for example, may be handled by up to three wholesalers, or the market gardener may carry out his own distribution by taking his produce to retail markets.

The main functions of wholesalers are as follows:

1. They simplify distribution by obtaining large orders from the main manufacturers and reselling to a large number of retailers.

Without their existence manufacturers would need to supply small orders to many retailers. An example showing the distribution of chocolate from producers to retailers with and without wholesalers is given below in Figure 7.

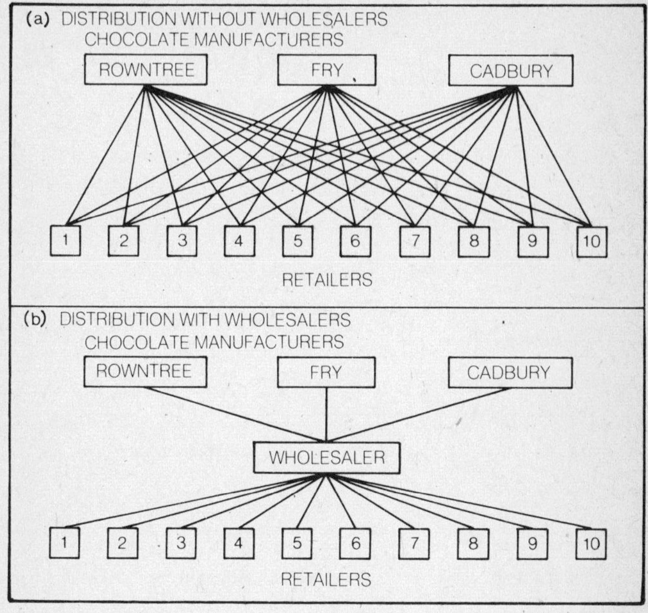

Figure 7. The wholesaler in distribution

2. Wholesalers hold large stocks, this aids the manufacturer and also helps the retailer who prefers to hold small stocks of many products. This function may also help to smooth out short-term fluctuations in price. Should prices rise the wholesaler can reduce stocks without raising the price of the goods to the retailer. When the price falls the wholesaler can restock.

3. Wholesalers can 'break-bulk'. Some commodities are sold by producers in quantities which are too large for an individual retailer. However, the wholesaler can purchase the commodity and resell in smaller quantities to the retailer. For example, dairies sell complete cheeses to wholesalers who divide them and sell smaller quantities of cheese to retailers.

4. Wholesalers provide an information channel between retailer and manufacturer. He can advertise and market goods to retailers on behalf of the producer, and can provide market information to the producer from the retailer.

5. Most wholesalers provide at least one specialist service, which may include providing credit facilities to the retailer, transportation, servicing of consumer durables, blending and packing (for example, some tea wholesalers also act as blenders of tea).

(C) Retailing

The characteristic of retailing is that the retailer acts as a link between a business unit on the one hand and the final consumer (usually the householder), on the other. In 1979 there were about 235,000 businesses in the retail trade with 351 outlets and they had a combined turnover of more than £52 billion.

The major functions of the retailer are as follows:

1. To stock small quantities of a wide range of products, thus providing the consumer with a good choice.
2. To provide a range of services to the consumer; marketing goods, maintaining showrooms, providing literature and generally advising the consumer to enable him to choose the product which would best suit the customer's purpose. Some retailers even allow 'trial periods', during which the consumer examines the product over a short period of time (usually between 5 and 14 days).
3. To provide an after-sales service. This may include servicing products or supplying extra or replacement parts, e.g. record shops usually sell record cleaners and record covers. Consumer protection legislation has increased the legal obligations of retailers with respect to after-sales service, and the replacement of faulty products is initially the responsibility of the retailer.
4. Many retailers provide their own credit facilities and credit accounts to enable the customer to pay over a period of time. Other retailers arrange credit for customers through finance houses which specialize in this type of lending.
5. To advise the wholesaler and manufacturer about customers' requirements, and their changes in tastes.
6. Some retailers provide a delivery service to their customers.

The structure of the retail trade. The structure of the retailing industry with respect to ownership and organization identifies several types of retailer.

1. Independents

Independent retailers are often shopkeepers with just one shop. However, independents are defined as retailers operating up to 9 small establishments. The most common example of the independent is the 'corner' or 'local' shop. The main advantages of the independents are that they tend to be conveniently located, and they often provide a friendly personal service. Their main disadvantage is that they are unable to buy in large quantities direct from the manufacturer at a discount rate and are thus forced to charge higher prices than the larger stores. In recent years voluntary organizations have been established (e.g. VG, Spar), whereby independents have combined to buy large quantities from manufacturers at lower prices.

Improvements in personal transport, and the development of the supermarket and hypermarket, (both of which are discussed in detail below), have considerably reduced the number of independent retailers, as consumers have sought lower prices. In 1950, there were over half a million independents, accounting for almost 70% of total retail sales. By 1980, the number of independents had fallen to about 200,000, and their share of trade to 30%.

2. Multiples

Multiples are retail organizations with at least ten establishments, and represent the attempts of the retail trade to obtain the advantages of large scale production techniques. The numbers of outlets and the share of retail trade taken by the multiples has expanded rapidly in post-war Britain. Multiples have tended to specialize in one product area, concentrating on selling large quantities of a limited number of lines. Examples can be found in many trades. Tesco and Sainsbury in the food trade; Burtons and John Colliers in men's tailoring; Ravel, Peter Lord, Dolcis and K Shoes in shoe retailing; Dewhursts in meat; Laskys in hi-fi and stereo equipment. The great advantage of the multiples is their ability to charge low prices as they buy in such large quantities from manufacturers at discount rates.

There are some multiples, known as 'variety multiples' which do not specialize to such an extent, Marks and Spencer and British Home Stores being two prime examples. In recent years the multiples have tended to diversify. Tesco, for example, now sell electrical goods, hardware, clothing and furniture, and are now installing bakeries in their larger stores.

3. Retail Cooperatives

In 1980 retail cooperatives accounted for 6·4% of total retail trade, much of this was in the food and grocery market. The first cooperative was set up in 1824, and the cooperatives grew steadily through the nineteenth and twentieth centuries. The rise of the multiples in the food trade after 1945 brought competition for the cooperatives. However, the cooperatives have managed to maintain their market share during the 1970s by the closing of smaller branches, the amalgamation of societies into larger groupings and the introduction of superstores and hypermarkets, which have brought the advantages of economies of scale.

4. Department stores

Department stores sell a wide range of products, including food, clothing, furniture, toys and games, cosmetics and electrical goods, furthermore they usually operate restaurants or cafeterias and encourage shoppers to buy all their requirements under one roof. In 1971 there were 818 department stores in Britain, 343 were owned by independents, 242 by multiples and 233 by co-operative societies. The centres of large towns are the most common sitings for department stores, as such stores need a large market to attract. It is not uncommon for two or more stores to compete in one town. Examples of department stores are Lewis's, Harrods, Selfridges, Fenwicks and Rackhams.

5. Mail order selling

Mail order selling has become increasingly popular since 1945. 1951 mail order sales amounted to only 1 per cent of total retail sales, but by 1979 this had increased to 4 per cent. Mail order firms tend to have most success in selling clothing, electrical goods and consumer durables; such firms also provide hire purchase facilities and normally allow their customers to pay over a period of time, normally 20 or 36 weeks.

6. Other forms of retailing

Other forms of retailing include mobile shops and market stalls, of which there were over 31,000 in 1971, and which specialize in selling foodstuffs. There are also over 500,000 vending machines in Britain which sell items such as cigarettes, sweets, drinks and postage stamps.

Recent developments in distribution

There have been several important developments in distribution during the past two decades. The three main changes have been the elimination of the middleman by manufacturers and retailers; the growth in the average size of retailing enterprises and establishments; the development of self-service stores. These three changes have not occurred separately, and frequently have been caused by a common factor; for example, the opening of a series of large self-service stores would encourage the retailer to by-pass the wholesaler, it would increase the average size of retailing establishment and would, of course, increase the total number of self-service stores.

1. The elimination of the middleman

Developments in manufacturing have been partly responsible for the elimination of the middleman in some product areas. The increasingly common practice for manufacturers to pre-pack some products has removed certain tasks previously undertaken by wholesalers. For example, cheese, bacon and eggs are frequently pre-packed today, whereas in the past, wholesalers would have carried out this function. On the retail side, the growth of large retailing establishments and of the introduction of large multiples into certain aspects of retailing (especially food), has meant that wholesalers have been eliminated as these large stores have dealt direct with manufacturers. Producers in some product areas have expanded their operations so as to enable them to carry out their own retailing. Breweries have taken over pubs to ensure that their own particular brand will continue to have retail outlets, and petroleum companies have acquired filling stations for the same reason. A rather more recent development has been the opening of 'discount warehouses'. This has been a successful venture of applying the techniques of multiple selling to consumer durables. Large stores with stocks of a limited range of products have entered the retailing industry in certain product areas, notably carpets (Allied Carpets); electrical appliances (Comet, Trident); furniture (M.F.I., Williams, Queensway). These enterprises buy huge quantities from manufacturers and obtain very large discounts and are thus able to charge low prices.

2. The growth of the average size of retailers

Both retail enterprises (i.e. firms), and retailing establishments (i.e. outlets), have grown in size. The improvements in transport have meant consumers have found it easier to visit town centres; large multiple organizations have found it easier than small retailers to obtain the finance to enable them to carry out extensive improvements and redevelopments, and this has driven the small retailers from town centre sites, to be replaced by large stores. A further factor which has increased the average size of retail outlets has been the increased application of new technology to retailing. Computers are now used to control the ordering of goods, cash flow, and even the number of checkouts open at different times of the day. Clearly such sophisticated equipment can reduce a firm's costs, but the small firm is unable to afford to purchase these labour saving devices, and thus is unable to obtain the economies of scale.

3. Self-service stores

Probably the greatest change in retailing has been the introduction of self-service stores. In 1961 there were only 9,500 stores operating on self-service lines, but by 1971 this number had risen to over 28,000. Self-service stores are often large, in which case they may be defined as either 'supermarkets' or 'superstores', depending on their size.

Supermarkets are defined as self-service stores having a minimum selling area of 100 sq. metres, in 1977 there were some 6,190 supermarkets in Britain. Supermarkets are usually found retailing in highly populated areas; their self-service techniques are mainly suitable for branded goods, which have been pre-packed and labelled, and which are sold in large quantities.

Superstores have a minimum selling area of 2,500 sq. metres. They usually stock a wide range of food and non-food goods, and have good parking facilities. Hypermarkets are basically the same, but have a minimum selling area of 5,000 sq. metres. The main advantages of superstores are that they sell a wide range of goods, usually at prices lower than their smaller competitors. Studies have suggested that superstores are up to 15% cheaper than smaller stores. Their major disadvantage is that they tend to be sited away from the traditional shopping centres, and thus customers have to pay extra transport costs to shop at them. By 1980 over 200 superstores and hypermarkets had opened and planning permission for a further 71 had been granted. Current Government policy is that such stores should be located within urban areas, preferably within shopping centres, where they are accessible to all shoppers including those without cars.

Advertising

Although the advertising industry does not undertake the distribution of goods, it aids the distributive process by providing information to consumers about products. In 1977 almost £1·5 billions was spent on advertising, representing 1·2% of gross national product. This represents a rise on previous years; from the mid 1950s to the mid 1970s advertising expenditure had been constant at about 1% of G.N.P.

According to the Advertising Association, advertising brings several advantages to the consumer including:
1. Increasing consumer knowledge on competing brands.
2. Encouraging manufacturers and retailers to keep their prices low in relation to their competitors.
3. Aiding the entry of new firms onto the market.
4. Increasing sales, which increases output and reduces unit cost, thus enabling manufacturers to charge lower prices.
The major disadvantages of advertising, put forward by various consumer groups, the Office of Fair Trading and the European Commission are that:
1. Some advertising encourages harmful practices, such as smoking and creates 'unsatisfiable wants' in vulnerable groups – such as children.
2. Advertising raises prices as firms engage in competition through their advertising campaigns (which raise costs), rather than competing on the prices they charge for their goods.

The advertising industry can be analysed by examining the four major groups involved.

1. Advertisers

The main advertisers are companies and government. However advertising expenditure by companies varies considerably from industry to industry.
The main advertisers are found to be in the product fields of food, household stores, toiletries and cosmetics, drink, motor vehicles and pharmaceuticals. When the Monopolies and Mergers Commission investigated the household detergent industry in the mid 1960s it was found that 23% of the average retail price of detergent was taken up by 'selling costs', i.e. advertising, promotions and market research.

2. Advertising agencies

There are about 700 advertising agencies in the U.K., and their main function is to organize advertising campaigns for the advertisers on a commission basis which brings in 70% of their revenue. They also charge advertisers for specialist services such as market research, the preparation of artwork, exhibition work and new product development, and this accounts for the remaining 30% of their revenue. Some agencies specialize in certain product areas, e.g. motor vehicles; others specialize in dealing with particular types of media, e.g. commercial radio.

3. Media owners

The main advertising media are the press and independent

television. Table 6, below shows the relative importance of the various media in 1964 and 1975.

Media	Percentage of total 1964	1975
National newspapers	21	17
Regional newspapers	23	29
Other press (magazines, etc.)	25	24
Total press	69	70
Television	25	25
Poster and Transport	4	3
Cinema	2	1
Radio	0	1
Total	100	100

Table 6. Advertising Media (1964 and 1975)

4. Ancillary services

Specialists are often used by advertisers, advertising agencies and the media to carry out various tasks and these include design consultants, photographers and cameramen, film producers and scriptwriters.

The control of advertising is carried out by the Advertising Standards Authority (ASA) through the Code of Advertising Practice (CAP). Both were set up in 1962. In 1976, over 2,000 complaints by the public concerning various advertisements were upheld.

Hire purchase

Hire purchase, or instalment credit as it is also known, became an important source of finance during the 1950s, enabling consumers to buy goods over a period of time. In 1977 credit up to £4,392 million was advanced by retailers and finance companies. Instalment credit is an important factor in the total sales of more expensive consumer durables, particularly motor vehicles, furniture, televisions, washing machines and other expensive electrical goods. Such credit is different to a loan as the retailers or finance company retain the ownership of the good until the last instalment has been paid. In recent years there has been a trend away from hire purchase, towards personal loans – in this case, if non-

payment occurs, the buyer retains the product and the lender has to use other means to obtain redress.
Controls on hire purchase and personal loans of this type exist in the form of regulations which specify the minimum deposit and the maximum period of repayment. Successive governments have changed these regulations to either stimulate or dampen demand.

Consumer protection

In the U.K. a wide range of legislation attempts to ensure that consumers' rights are safeguarded and their interests protected. Basic protection relating to weights and measures has existed since early times, but the majority of legislation has been introduced during the last twenty five years. Legislation pertaining to weights and measures was tightened up by the 1953 Merchandise Marks Act. The Food and Drugs Acts of 1955, 1956 and 1958 regulate the sale of food, drugs and medicines, ensuring a high degree of hygiene and quality. The Consumer Protection Acts of 1961 and 1971 prevent the sale of dangerous or harmful consumer goods. The increasing use of advertising during the 1960s brought with it some unfair methods of persuasion, and the 1968 Trade Descriptions Act made illegal misleading statements concerning a good or service, and the misrepresentation of prices. Several acts passed during the 1970s brought an increasing level of protection to consumers. In 1972 a ministerial post was created with special responsibility for consumer affairs and the 1973 Fair Trading Act established a Director General of Fair Trading whose tasks included the investigation of commercial activities that might adversely affect the interests of the consumer. The Director General can attempt to regulate such practices either through an order of Parliament or by proposing changes in the law. The 1973 Act also provides for the continuous review of consumer affairs. More recent legislation includes the Consumer Safety Act 1978 which empowers the Government to control the supply of any goods in the interests of consumer safety.
Consumer information and advice is available from several independent organizations including Citizens Advice Bureaux and Consumer Advice Centres. The views of consumers are represented to Government and industry by the National Consumer Council which is an independent body which receives government finance.
Consumers have attempted to protect themselves from unfair practices by setting up local consumer groups, and through the Consumers Association which has a membership of about

700,000. The Consumers Association promotes consumers' interests by acting as a pressure group, and by carrying out comparative tests on goods and services, the results of which are published in the monthly magazine 'Which'.

Key terms

The Distributive trade provides the connecting link between consumers and producers.
Independent retailers are defined as those retailers operating up to 9 small establishments.
Multiples are retail organizations with at least ten establishments.
Supermarkets are self-service stores having a minimum selling area of 100 sq. metres.
Superstores have a minimum selling area of 2,500 sq. metres.

Chapter 7
Location of Industry

A major decision of any business organization will be to decide upon the geographical location of production.

A wide variety of factors influence the decision to locate a plant, firm or industry. Problems in making such a decision exist because the importance of each of these factors to any firm changes over time, and the relative importance of any particular factor varies from firm to firm.

The major assumption concerning the location of a firm is that the entrepreneur will decide to operate at the 'least-cost' location. That is, he will wish to produce at that location where his costs per unit will be at a minimum.

Factors which influence the location of a firm

Major factors which determine how firms are sited and some of the reasons why are:

1. The supply of raw materials

A prime example of the need to locate at the site of the raw materials is the mining industry. A coal mine must be located at the site of the coal reserves. Other industries are also attracted to the source of their raw materials. The location of the cotton industry in Lancashire was clearly due to the high cost of transporting cotton away from the port of Manchester. Today the sugar-beet processing plants are located near to the beet fields because beet is expensive to transport, whereas the refined sugar is cheap to transport.

2. The proximity and size of the market

In some industries the cost of transporting the finished product is high, and in such a situation the firm will tend to locate near to the market. Bread and bricks are two finished products which are expensive to transport and so the bakeries and brickworks tend to be sited near to towns and cities. Firms which export a large proportion of their output will be attracted to the ports to reduce their transport costs. Clearly, firms which provide personal services such as hairdressers and shoe repairers will be attracted to the markets for their service – i.e. towns and cities.

3. Transport

Areas with good transport facilities can attract firms because transport costs can be reduced. The motorway system has encouraged firms to move from the large towns where travelling time (and thus cost) is increased due to traffic congestion.

4. Supply of power

The major industries of the nineteenth century – shipbuilding, textiles and woollens – were sited on or near the coal reserves because they all needed power which was supplied by coal. The availability of other forms of power (oil, gas, electricity), has meant that today, firms can locate almost anywhere in the country and obtain energy in plentiful quantities.

5. Supply of water

Some productive processes need large quantities of water in order to operate. Nuclear power stations, steel works and also chemical plants require large quantities of water and thus tend to be sited on the coast or by a river.

6. Labour

Firms need an adequate supply of suitable labour, and will not locate where output will be retarded by labour shortages. The concentration of skilled pottery workers in North Staffordshire provides a huge attraction for firms in this industry. In recent years entrepreneurs have appeared to avoid areas which have a reputation for poor industrial relations. Merseyside is one area which has seemed to suffer for this reason.

7. Land

Products which are manufactured on large assembly lines need large areas of flat land, and thus items such as motor vehicles will only be manufactured at certain locations.

8. The supply of components

The location of manufacturing processes which depend on a steady supply of component parts from other industries will be affected by the location of component industries. Car assembly firms find it cheaper to locate near to their component suppliers.

9. Waste disposal facilites

Legislation and pressure from environmentalist groups has meant that firms must pay more attention to their waste disposal, and this may affect their location decision. Some productive processes, such as the generation of electricity by nuclear power are dangerous or involve the production of dangerous by-products, and often need a site in areas of sparse population.

10. Government policy

Government may increase or reduce the cost of a particular site. For example, a new motorway will reduce the cost of some sites, whereas the raising of tax on diesel fuel would increase the cost of transport and thus make other sites more expensive. The protection of the countryside and of buildings of historical importance has completely excluded the possibility of locating on certain sites.

Concentrated and dispersed industries

Some industries are scattered throughout the country whereas others are concentrated in particular areas. The existence of a highly concentrated industry suggests that a region has important advantages for a particular form of production. A natural advantage may exist – such as the availability of raw materials (coal), convenient power supplies (textiles), or a concentrated market (consumer durables in and around London). Alternatively a region may acquire advantages over a period of years, such as a skilled labour force (pottery), component industries (motor vehicles), or the development of commercial and educational services (footwear in the East Midlands).

Dispersed industries are those where closeness to the market is of great importance – such as the service industries (retailing, the professions). The production of perishables tends to be dispersed as it is possible to have only a short time lag between production and consumption. The development of refrigerated lorries, better transport facilities, and the trend towards tinned and frozen foods has reduced the dispersion of some of these industries.

The regional problem

Although the concentration of an industry in an area can bring advantages in the form of lower costs and lower prices, it can also create severe problems. If the demand for the industry's output falls the effect will be felt in a small area and may result in high localized unemployment, Localized unemployment is a serious problem because workers in ancillary and component industries, those supplying personal services, and even shopkeepers may find themselves out of work, together with those from the concentrated industry. This may bring about the economic decline of the whole area.

The industries which had been successful in the nineteenth century – coal, shipbuilding, steel and textiles were concentrated in certain parts of the country; this had brought benefits to the whole country. However, the decline in the demand for their output which began after the First World War brought about high localized unemployment which continues to create severe problems even today.

The level of unemployment is a major determinant of prosperity and areas of high unemployment tend to be less prosperous than areas of low unemployment. During the inter-war years large regional variations were observed within the U.K. In 1932 the national rate was 22%, but this varied between 2% in parts of Surrey, to 75% in parts of South Wales and the North East. This regional imbalance was due to the falling demand for the output of the 'older' industries and nowadays is referred to as the **'Regional problem'.**

Traditionally governments had not interfered in industry and firms made location decisions based on their own criteria and preferences. However, the regional disparities were so serious that in 1934 government made its first attempt to obtain some sort of balance between the regions, but the measures taken had little effect. The Second World War saw full employment, but the Regional problem returned after 1945; the less prosperous regions of the 1930s became the less prosperous regions of the 1940s. Low national unemployment, and legislation aided the problem in the 1950s and early 1960s, but rising unemployment in the late 1960s saw an increase in regional disparities. The Regional Problem took on a new dimension during the 1979 recession. The British motor vehicles industry suffered a large decline in demand and the concentration of this industry in the West Midlands brought about a large rise in the unemployment rate in this region. For many years the unemployment rate in this region had been one of the lowest in the country, but by 1982 the rate was comparable with those in Wales and Scotland, traditionally two of the 'black-spots' of regional unemployment.

Region	Unemployment rate (%) 1966	1976	1982
North	2·5	7·6	16·3
Yorks and Humberside	1·1	5·6	13·2
East Midlands	1·0	4·9	11·0
East Anglia	1·4	4·9	10·4
South East	0·9	4·2	9·2
South West	1·7	6·5	10·9
West Midlands	0·8	5·9	15·2
North West	1·4	7·1	15·3
Wales	2·8	7·5	16·1
Scotland	2·7	7·0	14·8
Northern Ireland	5·9	10·3	19·5
United Kingdom (Average)	1·5	5·8	12·6

Table 7. U.K. Regional unemployment rates (1966, 1976 and 1982)

Regional policy in the U.K.

The 1972 Industry Act forms the basis of U.K. Regional policy although it is supported by other legislation.

Various governments have tended to follow two approaches to the problem. Firstly, workers have been encouraged to move from the areas of high unemployment to the areas of low unemployment. Secondly, governments have sought to increase employment opportunities in the less prosperous regions. This has been carried out in three ways:

(a) By providing financial assistance to aid the modernization and development of firms already located in these areas.

(b) By encouraging firms to move to the less prosperous regions, thus increasing employment.

(c) By improving the infrastructure of the high unemployment areas, so making them more attractive to business.

The first approach of moving workers to the work, is supported by various schemes, administered by the Manpower Services Commission, whereby the unemployed can receive grants and allowances of up to £100 to enable them to take up jobs in other areas, to attend interviews, or to move to other areas temporarily to seek work.

Incentives to firms

The second approach is the more favoured one, and several financial incentives and controls encourage the development of industry in the less prosperous areas. The overall strategy is to reduce the cost to firms of locating in the areas of high unemployment, whilst making location elsewhere difficult. The 'Depressed areas' (as they are also known), are divided into three categories which qualify for various forms of assistance. The criteria for designating an 'Assisted Area' are the level of unemployment, the rate of population decline and the rate of economic growth. Figure 8 shows the location of these areas, and the assistance available to firms is specified below.

Special development areas (S.D.A.s)

These are areas where economic improvements are most urgently required due to very high rates of unemployment. An example can illustrate the seriousness of the problem. Assistance available to firms includes a grant to cover 22% of the cost of new building, works, machinery and plant, plus free rent for up to 7 years.

Development areas (D.A.s)

These are areas of high unemployment where at least one major industry is in decline. Firms setting up in these areas receive up to 20% of the cost of new buildings, works, machinery and plant, and free rent for up to 5 years.

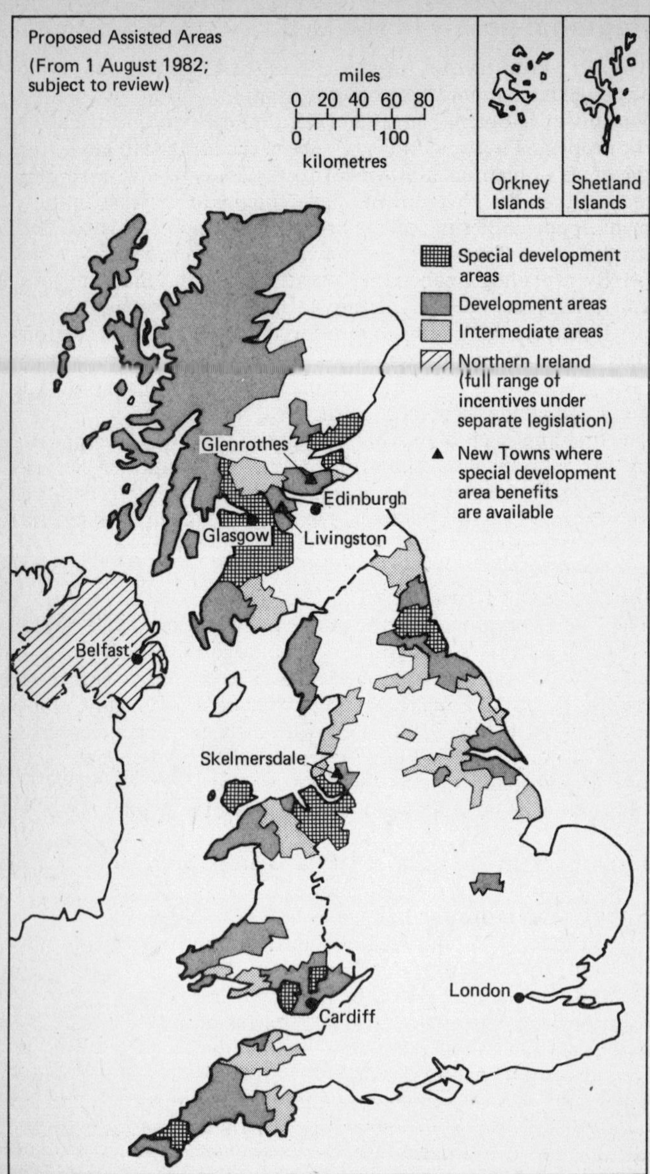

Figure 8. The Assisted Area (1 August 1982).

Intermediate areas

Some areas have been designated Intermediate areas as they were able to offer neither the advantages of the prosperous areas nor the financial benefits of the Development areas. In the Intermediate areas firms can receive up to 20% of the cost of new buildings and works only, and free rent for up to 3 years. Other financial assistance in the form of loans, grants and removal grants is available in all assisted areas, but this is usually dependent upon the number of new jobs created.

Development controls

Controls on development exist in certain parts of the country. Industrial Development Certificates (I.D.C.s) are required for developments of more than 5,000 sq. ft. in the South East, of more than 10,000 sq. ft. in the other non-assisted areas and of 15,000 sq. ft. in the Intermediate areas. I.D.C.s are not required for developments in the Development areas and the Special Development areas. By reducing the number of I.D.C.s granted the government can encourage firms to carry out their developments in the assisted areas.

Other policies include the Location of Offices Bureau brief, which since 1977 has been encouraging firms to move their offices out of the city centres. The government has also taken an active lead in supporting regional policy by re-locating some of its offices in the Development areas. The Department of Health and Social Security has its headquarters in Newcastle-upon-Tyne; the Driving Licence Centre is located in Swansea.

Enterprise zones

The Conservative government (1979–) has designated eleven areas as 'enterprise zones' (in London's docklands, Swansea, Salford/Trafford, Corby, Dudley, Hartlepool, Wakefield, Liverpool, Newcastle/Gateshead, Clydebank and Belfast) in an attempt to bring new life to areas of urban decay and where unemployment rates are highest. Firms established in the zones are exempt from DLT and general rates, they receive certain tax benefits and enjoy simplified planning procedures. The government hopes that these zones will attract new and existing firms and help to ease the worst of the regional disparities.

New towns

Since 1946, 32 new towns have been designated (21 in England, 2 in Wales, 5 in Scotland, 4 in Northern Ireland), and they now have a population of over 2 millions. The new towns have been planned to help the dispersal of industry and population from congested conurbations, and to act as growth points. Some of the new towns have already suffered from high rates of unemployment and others have found some difficulty in obtaining a balance of industry. In Stevenage, for example, 30% of the employed work for English Electric. A further problem is that some people have continued to work in the conurbations and commute from the new towns.

The effectiveness of regional policy

It is very difficult to examine how effective regional policy has been in reducing the imbalances in prosperity between the regions. Supporters of regional policy point to the amount of finance which has been taken up by firms in carrying out developments in the assisted areas. Certainly there does not appear to have been any widening in the gap between the more and less prosperous regions of the U.K. A further point is that the employment opportunities in the depressed areas would almost certainly diminish if the assistance available to firms was curtailed. Critics of present regional policy suggest that the types of assistance which are available to firms attract capital intensive industry rather than labour intensive industry, and thus the size of government assistance to firms for each job created has been colossal. One development in Scotland has cost the taxpayer £1 million for every new job created. The controls on developments in the rest of the country through the I.D.C.s has also been heavily criticised; it is suggested that firms which are not granted an I.D.C. simply abandon their investment plans, and thus the whole nation suffers.

The overall opinion of regional policy is that although its success or failure is difficult to measure it has been very expensive to operate but without it the regional imbalances would be even greater than they are today.

Key terms

Concentrated industries are those concentrated in relatively small areas.

Dispersed industries are those scattered throughout the country.

The Regional problem refers to the regional imbalances in prosperity, caused mainly by variations in unemployment rates.

Assisted areas are those areas of the country which qualify for government assistance designed to reduce regional unemployment.

Chapter 8
Population

Population can be defined as the total number of inhabitants of a particular place or area. The study of human populations is called demography.

1. The importance of population

A study of population is of great importance to the economist, for economics is a study of how mankind allocates scarce resources amongst unlimited wants. But, population determines both the demand for these scarce resources, and the total supply of resources available. In short, each person provides a pair of hands to work with, and a mouth to feed.

Many nations carry out extensive population studies because to complete a simple head count to determine present needs is insufficient. Rather, nations wish to know of future demands, and of the future supply of individuals who will be available to work so as to help provide the necessary resources.

To illustrate the need for such studies, suppose that the population of the United Kingdom is increasing because more births are taking place. This means the country must increase its food supplies to feed these extra mouths. The nation will also require more nurseries, more schools and more hospitals; these institutions will need more doctors, nurses and teachers. However, it takes many years to build such places, and more builders, electricians and plumbers will be needed before this can be done. If we look even further ahead we can predict that more jobs will have to be created and houses built, to ensure people are not left unemployed or homeless. It can be seen that if the nation is to cope with this increase in population it must carry out studies on which plans can be formulated to guarantee that the resources are available for the community.

This simple example shows just how important it is for a nation to carry out population studies so that effective planning for the future can take place.

2. How population changes

Changes in the size of a nation's population depend on three factors (i) the number of births, (ii) the number of deaths (iii) the number entering and leaving the country.

The number of births is measured by the **Birth rate,** which is the number of live births per thousand of population per annum. There are two major factors which determine the birth rate. Firstly, the number of women of child-bearing age (this is normally taken as 15 to 44 years, although the large majority of births occur to women in the age group 20 to 29). Secondly, the number of children born to women during this child-bearing period. The first factor is determined by the birth rates of previous years. The second factor, the number of children born to each woman, is influenced by many things which include, **(a) marriage** Increases in the number of marriages would tend to increase the birth rate whereas a decrease in the number of marriages would tend to decrease the birth rate. Another important point is that the higher the average age of marriage the lower will be the birth rate because the number of years within the child-bearing period is reduced.

(b) The cost of raising children If the cost of raising children increases, the birth rate would tend to fall. A reduction in the cost of raising children would tend to increase the birth rate.

(c) Birth control and abortion An increase in the use of birth control or in the number of abortions performed would tend to decrease the birth rate. The extent of such practices is often influenced by social customs and religious beliefs. In the Republic of Ireland, for example, where the birth rate is the highest in Europe, abortion is rarely performed and certain forms of birth control are illegal.

(d) Job opportunity for women If job opportunities for women improved, the birth rate would tend to fall, partly because some women might wish to concentrate on their careers and bear fewer children, and also because the necessity to give up work would increase the cost of raising a child.

(e) Government policy Action by governments can influence the birth rate. Changes in the cost of raising children can be brought about by changes in child benefit allowances and maternity benefits. Birth control and abortion can be made more or less accessible, and even the age of marriage can be influenced – the Chinese government strongly supports late marriage amongst the Chinese population, as a method of reducing the birth rate.

The number of deaths is measured by the **Death rate,** which is the number of deaths per thousand of population per annum. A high death rate (e.g. 30 per thousand) indicates that the average life expectancy is low, whereas a low death rate (e.g. 10 per thousand) indicates that the average life expectancy is high. The main factors which influence the death rate are as follows:

(a) The standard of living A high standard of living, with good food and housing will increase life expectancy and lower the death rate.

(b) Medical knowledge Advancements in medical knowledge, and the use of such developments will tend to reduce the death rate.

(c) Public health services Improvements in supplies of clean, uncontaminated water, the construction of sewage systems, and the introduction of refuse disposal and street cleaning can lead to a fall in the death rate by reducing incidences of disease, in particular cholera and typhus. Vaccination against the major infectious diseases, such as diptheria and smallpox, and mass X-ray campaigns to combat tuberculosis will also reduce the death rate.

If the Birth rate exceeds the Death rate it is said that there has been a natural increase in population.

The third factor affecting a country's population is the number entering the country (immigration), and the number leaving the country (emigration). The balance of the two is termed (net) **Migration.** If emigration has exceeded immigration, net migration is negative. Net migration is positive when immigration has exceeded emigration. Migration can be expressed as the Net Migration rate, which is net migration per thousand of population per annum.

Once the total number of births, deaths and migration have been calculated, the change in a country's population can be obtained.

3. Theories of population

The first major theory of population was put forward in 1798 by the Rev. Thomas Malthus in his '*Essay on Population*'. Malthus observed that population was ultimately limited by the supply of food. He suggested improvements in food supply would lead to an increase in the standard of living, which would lead to earlier marriage and more births; this would decrease the standard of living towards a subsistence level. Malthus believed that the population would tend to increase faster than the increases in food supplies and that this would lead to famine, misery, war and poverty. If disaster was to be avoided preventive checks would

have to be made to reduce the birth rate, particularly later marriage. Malthus disapproved of birth control.
The United Kingdom, and other Western European nations did not suffer the fate predicted by Malthus for the following reasons. Firstly, rising living standards of the last century have, in fact seen a falling birth rate. Secondly, Malthus did not anticipate the large increases in the food supply due to the application of new technology to farming, and also to the improvements in transport which meant that large quantities of food could be obtained from the new continents.

The second major theory of population was introduced in 1888, by Edwin Cannon, and is the 'theory of optimum population'. A nation's optimum population is that population where, with the existing level of economic resources, output per man is at a maximum. Such a situation would create an expanding output and real increases in living standards. This is shown at population level P_1 in Figure 9 below.
With a smaller than optimum population, the nation's economic resources would be underutilized, the scope for specialization would be limited, and this would lead to an artificially low standard of living. Such a situation is described as 'underpopulation', and is shown in Figure 9.

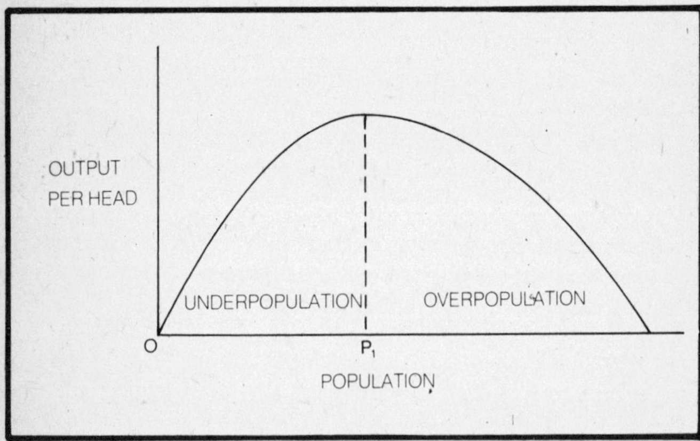

Figure 9. The concept of optimum population

Overpopulation exists where the population cannot be sustained with the existing level of resources. Output per man is low as each worker only has a small amount of land and capital at his disposal. This low output means that living standards will be low. Furthermore high unemployment is likely to be present, with all its various problems.

It can now be seen that in terms of Cannon's theory, the theory of population put forward by Malthus was in fact a theory of overpopulation – where population is too great for the nation's resources.

4. The British population

A Census of population (a full official population count) has taken place in the United Kingdom every ten years since 1801, with the exception of the war year 1941. The most recent census was carried out in 1971, and attempted to obtain information on a wide range of social, demographic and economic factors which could provide a sound basis for economic and social planning. The Census asked 29 questions of every household in the U.K. on a wide range of issues. The returns provided valuable statistics which were required for planning and research in education and training, housing, health and transport. Other information relating to average family size and the average age of marriage was also available.

The Census, together with the information from the compulsory registration of births, marriages and deaths provides large quantities of reliable information concerning the population of the U.K.

The growth of the U.K. population

Year	Population (millions)
1701	6·0 estimate
1801	11·0 (excluding N. Ireland)
1851	22·3
1901	38·2
1921	44·0
1941	48·2
1961	52·7
1971	55·6
1980	55·9
2001	57·5 projection

Table 8. United Kingdom Population

The history of the U.K. population can be analysed in four time periods.

1. Pre 1801 The population of the United Kingdom grew very slowly during the Middle Ages, birth rates and death rates were high and average life expectancy was low – about 30 years. During the eighteenth century the population doubled due to a rising birth rate (from 31 per thousand in 1700 to 38 per thousand in 1781), and a decrease in the death rate after 1741. Probably both changes were brought about by the improvements in living standards. The Agrarian revolution improved food supplies, increased employment and raised wages. The Agrarian revolution was followed by the Industrial revolution which also raised standards. Improvements in transport (particularly the railways and canals) reduced the prices of many commodities, and the developments in the textile and woollen industries meant that cheaper clothing was available. These improvements in living standards decreased the average age of marriage, and the increasing demand for child labour reduced the cost of raising children; the birth rate rose accordingly. The increased food supplies and improvements in hygiene together with better clothing increased life expectancy and thus reduced the death rate.
By 1801 the birth rate was 37 per thousand, the death rate was 27 per thousand, and the population was increasing by 1% each year.

2. 1801–1911 The population doubled in the first half of the century, from 11 millions in 1801 to 22·3 millions in 1851, and almost doubled in the second half of the century – to 38·3 millions in 1901. The main reason for this increase can be seen in a falling death rate and a constant birth rate. By 1851 the death rate had fallen to 22·7 per thousand, fifty years later it was 14 per thousand. Several factors contributed to this fall, these included:
(a) continuing improvements in diet and personal hygiene,
(b) advancements in medical knowledge,
(c) the increased provision of public health services and sanitation.
The birth rate remained at a high level until it began to fall after 1881. By 1911 it had fallen to 25 per thousand. The reasons for this can be seen partly in the increased cost of raising children, as child labour was made illegal and compulsory schooling was introduced. Another factor was that families began domestic expenditure on consumer goods and increased leisure rather than having more children. By the beginning of the twentieth century the rate of population growth had slowed down considerably to ½% per annum.

3. 1911–1941 The birth rate continued to decline apart from a post-war bulge, as husbands returned home, and marriages delayed by the war took place. The following factors were responsible for this falling birth rate:
(a) The increased use of improved birth control methods, which became readily available and socially acceptable.
(b) The death of 745,000 younger men during the war, which had changed the balance between the sexes, reduced the number of marriages and thus the birth rate.
(c) The increased employment opportunities for women.
Following the war, the death rate began to stabilize at about 15 per thousand, as can be seen in Figure 10 below.

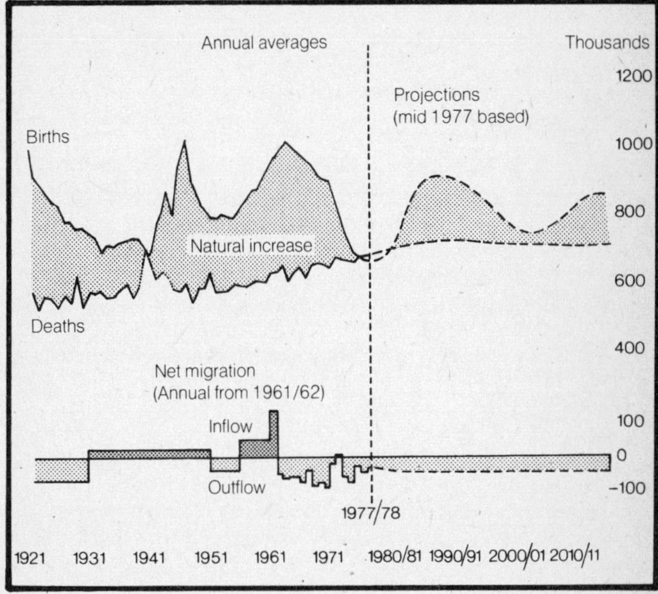

Figure 10. U.K. population changes and projections

A further factor which affected the U.K. population during this period was migration. Prior to 1931, the losses due to emigration had been greater than the inflows of immigrants, but the 1930s saw a reduction in emigration on account of the depression and a large inflow of refugees from Europe.
There was great concern about the possibility of a declining popu-

lation, caused by the falling birth rate. In 1935, for example, the Chancellor, Neville Chamberlain expressed 'considerable apprehension' about the situation, and increased family allowances to reduce the cost of raising children.

4. The post-war period. During the post-war period the death rate has remained fairly stable. The most notable point has been the changing structure of deaths. The infant mortality rate (i.e. perinatal deaths – stillborn and first week deaths) have decreased substantially from 30 per thousand live births in 1950 to only 17 per thousand in 1977. The causes of death have also changed dramatically. In the middle of the nineteenth century the chief causes of death were the major infectious diseases, such as diphtheria and whooping cough together with tuberculosis and typhoid – diseases associated with poor diet and poor sanitation. However, the major killers in 1977 were cancer, which caused one fifth of all deaths, and various circulatory diseases (particularly heart attacks and strokes) which account for almost 40% of deaths.

The birth rate has fluctuated widely since 1941. In 1942 the birth rate increased sharply and by 1947 had risen to 20·7 per thousand. But, in 1948 the rate began to decline once again, and fears of a declining population precipitated the setting up of the Royal Commission on Population in 1949. In the late 1950s the birth rate began to rise again, reaching a post-war peak of 20 per thousand in 1964. Since that time the birth rate has fallen steadily, and in 1977 was only 11·6 per thousand, in which year there was a natural decrease in population. The main reasons for these changes in the birth rate since the war are as follows:

(a) Family planning has become widespread. In recent years there has been a decline in the use of the less reliable forms of contraception, and an increase in the use of the more reliable forms – the pill and sterilization. Furthermore, the Abortion Act of 1967 permits the termination of pregnancy under certain conditions, and in 1977, 103 thousand legal abortions took place, about half of which were to married women.

(b) Couples have tended to choose a higher material standard of living rather than large families. Specifically, since the mid 1960s couples have tended to wait longer after marriage until having a first child; and the numbers of couples having more than two children has decreased substantially.

(c) The emancipation of women has continued. In 1951 only 20% of married women were in employment: by 1980 this figure had risen to 50%, and this trend is expected to continue. This has meant that an increasing number of women have opted to develop their careers rather than be mere child-bearers. A further point is that if the cost of raising a child increases should a woman need to give up her employment during and after pregnancy.

(d) The post-war peaks in the birth rate can be explained in social and economic terms. The first peak is related partly to the fact that this period saw an increase in the number of women of child-bearing age, and partly to the fact that the end of the war meant that war-delayed marriages took place. The second peak was caused primarily by large increases in the standard of living during the late 1950s. This increase in the living standard was caused by the very low level of unemployment, which averaged less than 1·5% from 1955 to 1960. When this is compared to the level of 12%, which operated in the 1930s, it is clear to see that many individuals were much better off during this period.

Migration has also had effects on the population of post-war Britain. During the late 1950s and early 1960s there was a substantial influx from the New Commonwealth, and for a short time immigration exceeded emigration. However the 1962 Commonwealth Immigrants Act reduced immigration, and there has been a net outflow since that time. Today there are approximately 3 million people born overseas, who are resident in Britain; of these a quarter were born in the Irish Republic, a third in various non-commonwealth foreign countries (in particular Europe and America) and the remaining 40% are from the Commonwealth Countries. It is expected that the current trend, of emigration exceeding immigration will continue.

The structure of the British population

It is possible to study the structure of the British population in several ways; in terms of the age distribution, the sex distribution, the geographical distribution and the occupational distribution.

The age distribution of the U.K. population

A study of the age distribution of a population can give a valuable insight into certain aspects of an economy. In particular, it gives the percentage of the population in the working age group (usually men 16 to 65, and women 16 to 60), and the number of people who are dependent on the working group, (i.e. children under 16, men over 65 and women over 60). The ratio of the working population to the dependent population is termed the dependency ratio.

The age distribution can be illustrated by the use of an age pyramid. The population is divided into various age groups, and the numbers in each group is plotted on a bar graph.

There are two main types of age pyramid, and these are shown in the following figure. The first, shown in Figure 11 (a) represents a country with a high birth rate and a high death rate. The proportion of young people will be high, but high mortality rates in all age groups will mean a low life expectancy, and only a small percentage of the population will reach old age. The second age pyramid shown in Figure 11 (b) represents a country with low birth rates and low death rates. More people survive to middle age and old age, and thus the proportion of young people is much lower than in the first case, above. The age structure of the British population today is of the second type, although a representation of the age distribution in 1800 would be of the first type.

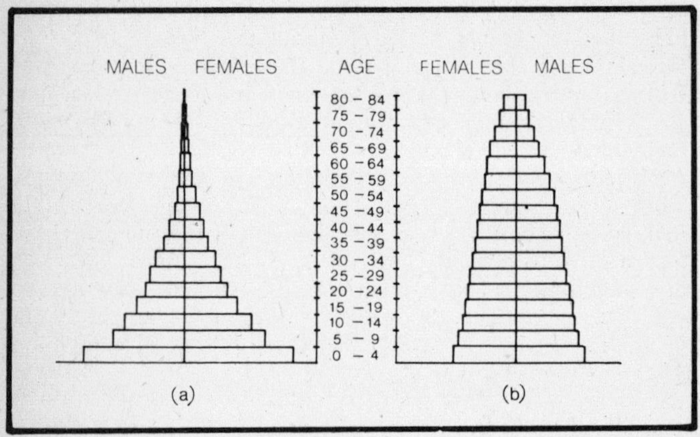

Figure 11. Age distribution pyramids

The dependency ratio is one of the most important statistics which becomes available from a study of the age distribution, as changes in this ratio can have considerable effects on the standard of living. However, changes in the age structure can have other consequences, one of which is the problem of **'an ageing population'**. This situation occurs when there are large numbers in the higher age groups. The numbers leaving the workforce and entering retirement may exceed the numbers of young people entering the workforce and thus a diminishing working population has to support an expanding dependent population.

A changing age structure is also likely to affect the pattern of demand and the mobility of labour. An ageing population would increase demand for such items as smaller homes and health care (as older people are more likely to require medical treatment). A rise in the birth rate would initially increase demand for push-chairs, baby foods and toys, and this would be followed by a rising demand for education and teenage products such as pop records, sports goods and magazines. A population with a low average age would be more prepared to change jobs and move homes, whereas an ageing population would be less mobile.

The age structure of the British population has undergone great changes during the twentieth century. In 1911, 31% of the population were under 15 years, 64% were aged 15 to 65, but only 5% were over 65. The falling birth and death rates meant that by 1977 the percentage under 16 had fallen to 24%, the percentage aged 16 to 65 was 63%, and those over 65 had risen to 13%. It is expected that the over 65 group will stabilize at about 14%, the under 16 group to fall to about 21%, and the 16 to 65 group to rise to 65%.

The sex distribution of the population

At birth, the ratio of males to females is 106:100, but a higher death rate in males means that females tend to exceed males from quite an early age. The information given in Table 9, below, illustrates this point.

Age	Males (millions)	Females (millions)
Under 15	6·1	5·7
15–64	17·9	17·9
65 and over	3·2	5·1
All Ages	27·2	28·7

Table 9. U.K. sex and age distribution (1980)

In the past, females exceeded males at an even earlier age than is the case today. For example, in 1921 there were 113 females to every 100 males in the 15 to 49 age group. The main reasons for this situation were (i) **Wars** – which reduced the number of males, particularly in the 15 to 49 age group. (ii) **The Armed Forces** – The British Empire required large numbers of men abroad, and this would affect the sex ratio at home. (iii)

Emigration – large numbers of young men emigrated to North America and Australasia during the late nineteenth and early twentieth century. The post-war period, with few wars causing the death of British males, and improved welfare services, has seen the natural ratio of males to females begin to establish itself in the higher age groups. In 1931 females began to exceed males at age 25, by 1971 females did not exceed males until age 45. By 2001 it is thought that males will continue to exceed females up to the age of 60. As the excess of females is reduced it can be expected that the number of marriages will increase, and this would tend to increase the birth rate.

The geographical distribution of the population

In the eighteenth century the British population was primarily located in the areas of good farming land. The major part of the population lived within a triangle which joined London, Bristol and Norwich.

The Industrial Revolution was responsible for a remarkable change in the geographical distribution of the population. The new industries of coal, iron and steel, textiles and woollens, engineering and shipbuilding were located in the areas of the coal reserves and thus large numbers of people moved to the new areas of employment and prosperity in the North of England. At the same time large scale immigration from Ireland and Scotland further increased the population of these areas.

The twentieth century saw a decline in these industries, which had been so successful during the nineteenth century. Improved transport facilities and availability of other energy sources reduced the need for firms to produce in the mining areas. The expanding industries of the twentieth century were light engineering, the manufacture of motor vehicles and consumer durables, and these were based in the Midlands and the South East. Once again large numbers migrated to find work, and today 25 million people live in these areas.

For the purposes of economic planning the U.K. is divided into 11 regions. There are 8 of these regions in England; Scotland; Wales; Northern Ireland. The planning regions are organized so that no region has a predominately rural population. The areas contained within each of these regions are shown in Figure 12, on the following page. The historical development of the U.K. population during the twentieth century is shown in Table 10.

Figure 12. The economic planning regions of the U.K.

Region	1911	1951	1977	1991 (projected)
Northern	2·8	3·1	3·1	3·1
Yorks and Humberside	3·9	4·5	4·9	4·9
East Midlands	2·3	2·9	3·7	4·0
East Anglia	1·2	1·4	1·8	2·1
South East	11·7	15·1	16·8	16·9
South West	2·7	3·2	4·3	4·7
West Midlands	3·3	4·4	5·2	5·3
North West	5·8	6·4	6·5	6·5
Wales	2·4	2·6	2·8	2·9
Scotland	4·8	5·1	5·2	5·2
Northern Ireland	1·2	1·4	1·5	1·5
United Kingdom	42·0	50·1	55·9	57·2

Table 10. The locational distribution of the U.K. population (millions)

The irregular geographical distribution of the population can be further illustrated by measuring the population density in the planning regions. The regions' population densities are shown in Table 11, below.

Region	Population density (persons per sq. mile)
Northern	417
Yorks and Humberside	890
East Midlands	797
East Anglia	375
South East	1590
South West	468
West Midlands	1025
North West	2112
Wales	349
Scotland	173
Northern Ireland	292
United Kingdom (Average)	598

Table 11. Population density in the U.K. (1980)

It can now be seen that the most densely populated areas are the North West and the South East, and that the least densely populated areas are Wales, Northern Ireland and Scotland.
In the United Kingdom almost eighty per cent of the population

lives in urban areas (i.e. towns and cities), and many of the 20% who live in the rural areas, work in the urban areas, so it can be seen that the U.K. is predominantly a nation of towns and cities. In fact, in 1977 there were six cities with more than 500,000 inhabitants, and a further thirteen with between 250,000 and 500,000 inhabitants. In the twentieth century the improvements in transport have aided the outward spread of the cities into the countryside, so that in some places large conurbations have been formed, where two or more towns have seemed to merge into one sprawling mass.

In the light of these developments, six Metropolitan counties were created as from 1st April 1974, which together with Greater London and Central Clydeside constitute the eight conurbations of the United Kingdom. The population of these conurbations is given in Table 12, below.

Conurbation	Population (millions)
Greater London	7·0
West Midlands	2·7
Greater Manchester	2·7
West Yorkshire	2·1
Central Clydeside	1·8
Merseyside	1·6
South Yorkshire	1·3
Tyne and Wear	1·2
Total contributions	20·3

Table 12. U.K. population in conurbations (1980)

The period 1961 to 1980 saw a fall of 6% in the population of these conurbations – a time when the total U.K. population increased by 6%. It is expected that this trend will continue, as more and more people leave the decaying city centres for the suburbs and the less congested areas. It is interesting to note that the main areas of population growth in the 1980s are projected to be the East Midlands and East Anglia.

The working population

In March 1982, the working population of the U.K. was 26·3 millions, which represents about 48% of the total population and almost 75% of the working-age group (men 16 to 65, women 16 to 60). The working population is given in Table 13.

Status	Millions
Employees in employment	21·1
Employers and self-employed	1·9
Unemployed	3·0
Armed Forces	0·3
Total working population	26·3

Table 13. The working population (March 1982)

In recent years there has been a rise in the population within the working-age group (see Figure 13a), and also a sizeable increase in the working population (see Figure 13b). This shows that more people of working age are seeking employment, and in particular, that there has been a large increase in the number of married women seeking gainful employment. In 1951 only 22% of married women were part of the working population, by 1977 this figure had risen to 50%, and it is expected that this will climb to 60% by 1991. The proportion of men in the working population of working age was 95% in 1951, but fell to 91% in 1977 and is expected to be 93% in 1991. The major reason for the fall in the number of males of working age in the working population has been the large increase in the number who have remained in full-time education after the school leaving age.

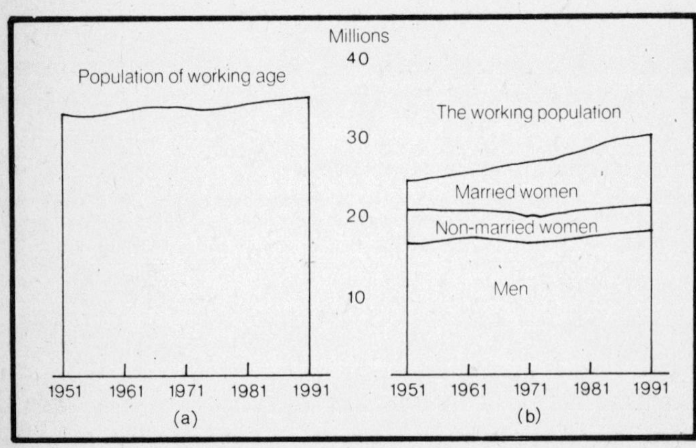

Figure 13. Changes in the labour force

The occupational distribution of the population

The occupational structure of the population was considered, in passing, when the locational distribution was examined. Internal migration has occurred, in the past, in answer to changes in the structure of industry. The Industrial Revolution changed not only the locational structure of the population, it also changed the occupational structure of the population. Agricultural workers had to change their trade and become miners, textile workers and engineers. The change in the structure of industry in the twentieth century has forced workers to again change trades, to become assemblers in car factories or bureaucrats in offices. Thus, changes in the structure of industry are reflected in changes of the occupation distribution of the population. Table 14 shows the occupational distribution of the U.K. population in 1971 and 1980.

	1971		1980	
Industry or Service	(000's)	Per cent	(000's)	Per cent
Primary Sector:				
Agriculture, forestry, fishing	734	3·1	637	2·6
Mining and quarrying	397	1·7	345	1·4
Manufacturing industries:				
Chemicals	483	2·0	471	1·9
Metal Manufacture	558	2·3	402	1·6
Textiles, leather, clothing	1,147	4·8	834	3·4
Engineering	3,650	15·2	3,151	12·9
Food, drink, tobacco	777	3·2	686	2·8
Other manufactures	1,565	6·5	1,383	5·7
Other production industries:				
Construction	1,594	6·6	1,651	6·8
Gas, electricity, water	377	1·6	347	1·4
Services:				
Transport and communications	1,639	6·8	1,578	6·5
Distributive trades	3,088	12·9	3,223	13·2
Professional, financial, scientific	6,512	27·1	8,094	33·2

contd.

Industry or Service	1971 (000's)	Per cent	1980 (000's)	Per cent
Government service	1,509	6·3	1,596	6·5
Total in civil employment	24,031		24,397	
of whom employees	22,122		22,511	
Self-employed	1,909		1,886	

Table 14. The occupational distribution of the U.K. population in 1971 and 1980.

Since 1900 there has been considerable change in occupational structure. Employment in the Primary industries (agriculture, fishing, mining) has fallen considerably, mainly due to greater mechanization. Total employment in the Secondary industries has remained fairly stable although the distribution of employment within this sector has changed. There has been a movement out of the 'older' industries, such as shipbuilding and textiles, and into the 'newer' industries such as the production of electrical goods. There has been a large increase in the numbers employed in the service industries, particularly banking, education and health care. A major problem associated with many of today's expanding industries is that large increases in production can be obtained with no increase in employment. For example, the chemicals industry, which is one of Britain's most successful industries, has seen a drop in employment while production has expanded due to the new and advanced production techniques. Should this occur in many industries the threat of widespread unemployment will become a reality, and the new technology associated with the silicon chip is expected to have a large effect on jobs.

5. World Population

Year	Population (millions)
1800	978
1850	1262
1900	1650
1950	2486
1970	3632
2000	(projected) 6494

Table 15. World population (1800–2000)

The world's population is expanding at a rate of 2% per annum. History reveals two booms in world population growth. The first occurred in Western Europe and was precipitated by the Agrarian and Industrial Revolutions. Large increases in living standards lowered the death rate and increased the birth rate resulting in a rapidly expanding population. After a period of about eighty years the birth rate and death rate stabilized at a relatively low level – as occurred in Britain, and the population growth slowed down considerably. The transition period between the original fall in death rates, which began the population boom, and a fall in birth rates to a level equal to the death rate, which ended the boom is termed the **demographic transition.** The second boom in population growth began about 20 years ago and is taking place in the developing countries, where the use of medical knowledge and improvements in sanitation have reduced the death rate to about 15 per thousand, but where birth rates remain high, at about 40 per thousand. However, this second population boom has preceded the improvements in agricultural productivity, and with malnutrition already widespread the prospects for some nations are rather bleak. The possible solutions include measures to reduce the birth rate and to increase agricultural productivity as quickly as possible. However, success in these areas, up to the present, has been very limited and many people believe that the developing nations will not reach population stability for a hundred years.

Key terms

The **Birth rate** is the number of live births per thousand of population per annum.
The **Death rate** is the number of deaths per thousand of population per annum.
Net Migration is immigration minus emigration, per annum.
The **Dependency ratio** is the ratio of the working population to the dependent population.
The Working population is the sum of: Those employees in employment, employers and the self-employed, the unemployed, and the Armed Forces.
The Demographic transition is that period of time, between the original fall in death rates, which begins a population boom, and the fall in birth rates to a level equal to the death rate, which ends the boom.

Chapter 9
The Price System

In a market economy, resources are allocated through a system of prices. If the price of a good rises, manufacturers will be encouraged to make this good, and resources will be diverted to the production of this good and away from other goods. In this way the price of the good has determined the volume of economic resources used in its production.

In a market economy the price of every good is determined in an individual market, by the forces of supply and demand. In order to understand how prices are determined in these individual markets for goods and services it is necessary to examine markets, supply and demand.

Markets

In economics, a market is a place or an area where buyers and sellers are in contact with one another, for the purposes of trading a particular good or service, and of fixing prices. Buyers demand the good and offer money in exchange. Sellers supply the good or service and receive money in exchange. In everyday speech a market usually refers to a local retail market where many different goods and services are traded, but in discussing the market in economics, a market for a particular good or service is examined, such as the market for washing machines, or the market for tin, or the market for combine harvesters.

An important point to note is that although a market is defined as a place or area where buyers and sellers are in contact, they can, of course, be in contact without meeting at a particular place, but by using the telephone and other communications systems such as telex. The markets for some goods are worldwide and it would be impossible for buyers and sellers to meet at one place; this does not prevent trading, and therefore this type of trading is a market according to the economist's definition.

Demand

As a factor determining price, demand is defined as the willingness to buy a good or service backed by the ability to pay for it. There are three points to note about demand:

1. Only 'effective' demand is considered to play a part in the determination of price, thus even though a person might like to

buy a Rolls Royce motor car, he will not be considered to form an effective demand unless he can afford the £30,000 he will require to pay for it.

2. Demand refers to demand at a particular price. So the demand for fresh tomatoes in the United Kingdom might be 500,000 kilos at a price of 35 pence per kilo.

3. Demand refers to demand per period of time. Thus the demand for fresh tomatoes in the United Kingdom might be 500,000 kilos at a price of 35 pence per kilo, per month.

Individual demand schedules

In examining the demand for fresh tomatoes per month, it would be possible to interview individual consumers concerning their demand for tomatoes. They could be asked to estimate their own demand for tomatoes per month at various prices, e.g. 20p per kilo, 60p per kilo, and so on. The main proviso is that all other factors which determine their demand for tomatoes, except price, must remain the same, for only in this way can the relationship between demand and price be examined. Clearly, factors other than price will determine an individual's demand for tomatoes. If a report was issued by the Department of Health that tomatoes could cause cancer then the demand for tomatoes could be expected to fall. If this change in consumers' demand was included, as well as the effect that different prices have on consumers' demand, then it would be impossible to determine whether a particular change in demand had been caused by a change in price or by the Health Department's report.

The returns from three imaginary consumers, concerning their demand for tomatoes might be as follows:

Price	Demand (kilos) per month		
(pence)	Individual A	Individual B	Individual C
70	2	0	1
60	3	0	1
50	5	1	2
40	7	2	3
30	10	4	5
20	13	6	7
10	17	8	9

Table 16. Individual demand schedule for tomatoes

From the table above we can make certain conclusions, firstly that Individual A has a far greater demand for tomatoes than Individuals B and C. Secondly, and much more important, that as the price of tomatoes falls all three individuals wish to buy more tomatoes.

The second conclusion, that a lower price results in a higher quantity being demanded is a typical response for almost all goods and services. If the price of butter falls, for example, people can be expected to buy more butter, and perhaps less margarine. If the price of petrol rises on the other hand, people will tend to buy less petrol, and will travel by rail and air. Thus price and demand have an inverse relationship, that is, as price rises demand falls, and as price falls demand rises.

Market demand schedules

It is theoretically possible to interview all the consumers who form an effective demand for a good or service, as in our example, tomatoes. The total demand for tomatoes at each price can be obtained by adding together the demand of all the individuals, to form a market demand schedule, which represents the total demand for tomatoes per month in the United Kingdom, at various prices.

Price (pence)	Demand (kilos per month)
70	100,000
60	150,000
50	250,000
40	400,000
30	550,000
20	700,000
10	900,000

Table 17. Market demand schedule for tomatoes (per month)

This schedule indicates the relationship between the price of tomatoes, and the demand for tomatoes, expressed in kilos per month. Thus, at a price of 70p, consumers would wish to buy 100,000 kilos of tomatoes per month; at a price of 60p they would wish to buy 150,000 kilos of tomatoes, and so on.

Market demand curve

The market demand schedule can be represented graphically by a market demand curve. Figure 14 shows a market demand curve for tomatoes, and the shape of this curve is typical of most demand curves, in that it slopes downwards from left to right, indicating that as the price falls the quantity demanded by consumers increases, and as the price rises the quantity demanded by the consumers decreases.

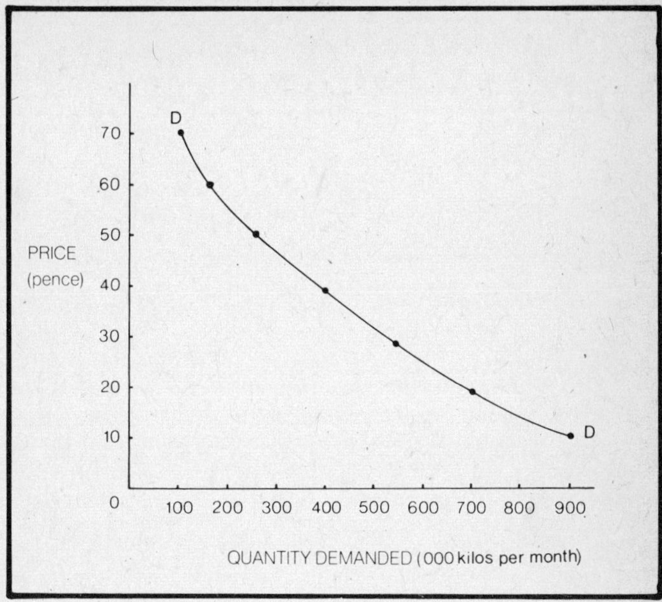

Figure 14. A market demand curve for tomatoes.

Changes in demand

Although the quantity demanded by consumers changes as the price they have to pay changes, the underlying conditions of demand are unaltered, and these price changes only cause movements on the demand curve. For example, if prices of tomatoes fell from 70p per kilo to 50p per kilo, then the quantity demanded would increase from 100,000 kilos per month to 250,000 kilos per month. There would simply be a movement along the demand curve.

However, suppose the Health department announced that eating tomatoes could cause cancer, it is most likely that fewer tomatoes would be demanded at every price, and this would involve not just a movement along the curve, but a shift of the complete curve, because the market demand schedule would indicate large reductions in the amount of tomatoes that consumers would wish to purchase. The new market demand schedule might be as follows:

Price (pence)	Demand (kilos per month)
70	0
60	0
50	0
40	150,000
30	300,000
20	450,000
10	650,000

Table 18. A decrease in demand for tomatoes.

On the other hand, the Health department could have issued a report stating that the eating of tomatoes was very good for a person's health, and that people who ate tomatoes tended to live longer. The effect of this statement might be expected to have the effect of increasing consumers' demand for tomatoes, so that at every price they are prepared to purchase more tomatoes. In this case the market demand schedule might be as follows:

Price (pence)	Demand (kilos per month)
70	325,000
60	375,000
50	475,000
40	625,000
30	775,000
20	925,000
10	1125,000

Table 19. An increase in the demand for tomatoes.

The changes in the demand schedules caused by two imaginary reports issued by the Health department can be represented graphically. Figure 15 shows the original demand curve, denoted DD; the demand curve D_1D_1 represents the fall in demand caused by the 'cancer' report; D_2D_2 represents the increase in demand caused by the report that eating tomatoes was good for the health.

It can be seen that a fall in demand has caused the demand curve to shift to the left, from DD to D_1D_1, indicating that at every price, fewer tomatoes are demanded. The rise in demand has made the demand curve shift to the right, from DD to D_2D_2, indicating that at every price, more tomatoes are demanded.

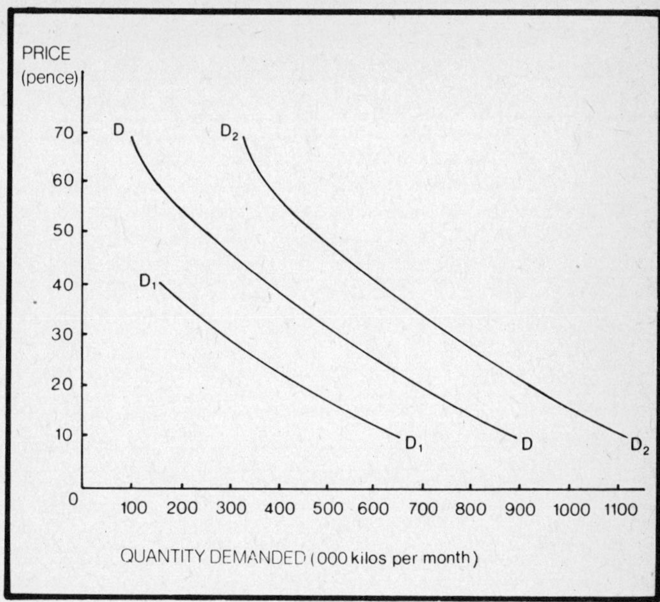

Figure 15. Shifts in the demand curve caused by changes in the conditions of demand.

The conditions of demand

The shifts in the demand curve have had nothing to do with the price of tomatoes, rather it has been the underlying conditions of demand that have been changed. A shift of the demand curve to the left indicates that the conditions of demand have changed so that people wish to buy fewer tomatoes, whereas a shift in the demand curve to the right indicates that people wish to buy more tomatoes, and that the conditions of demand have changed in favour of buying tomatoes.

The conditions of demand, not only for tomatoes, but for all goods and services, are as follows.

1. The prices of other goods. If the price of other goods change the demand for a good or service can also change. In the case of tomatoes, if the price of other salad foods falls, then more tomatoes may be demanded, at all prices, if consumers begin to eat more salads. A rise in the prices of other salads might reduce the demand for tomatoes if people decided to eat fewer salads. If a rise in the price of one good causes the demand for another good to fall the goods are said to have a joint demand. Examples of joint demand include cars and petrol, where if the price of petrol rises the demand for cars can be expected to fall.

If the rise in the price of one good causes the demand for another good to rise, this indicates that the goods are substitutes. For example, if the price of tea rises, then it can be expected that the demand for coffee will rise since people will drink more coffee and less tea. Other examples of substitutes are margarine and butter, road travel and rail travel, heating by gas and electricity; in all these cases if the price of one of the goods were to rise, then the demand for the other could be expected to rise.

2. The real income of consumers. If the real income of consumers falls, then the demand for all products can normally be expected to fall. For example, if levels of income tax rise, consumers will have a smaller level of income to spend on goods and services, and the demand curve for goods can be expected to move to the left. An increase in consumers real income will normally shift the demand curve to the right.

3. Tastes and fashions. The tastes of consumers vary, and these changes can cause the demand curve to shift to the right or the left. Some changes in taste occur over a long period of time, for example the demand for fountain pens has fallen slowly over the years since the introduction of the ball point pen in 1945. The change in taste away from fountain pens has in effect moved the demand curve for fountain pens to the left. Some changes in taste are only temporary; this is often the case with a particular fashion, such as wearing cords rather than jeans, where in one year people will prefer to wear cords and the next year they prefer to wear jeans, but there is no long-term trend in favour of either one or the other. Changes in fashions will shift the demand curve of the favoured product to the right, indicating that more will be demanded at all prices.

4. Advertising. The basic aim of advertising is to persuade the consumer to buy more of a particular commodity at all prices, that is, to shift the demand curve to the right.

5. Population. An increase in population will tend to increase the demand for all products and will thus shift the demand curve to the right. A decrease in population will tend to shift the demand curve to the left. The age distribution of the population will also effect the demand for certain products. A population which includes many young people will demand more toys and teenage

products, whereas an ageing population will demand more health care, and more walking sticks.
A change in the conditions of demand for a product will either shift the demand curve to the right (if the change has been in favour of the product), or will shift the demand curve to the left (if the change has been away from the product).

Supply

The supply of a commodity is that quantity that sellers are prepared to sell at a given price. The most important factor determining the amount that sellers are prepared to sell is the price of the product. For example, if a market gardener believes that he will obtain a high price for tomatoes he will grow as many tomatoes as he can, so that he will obtain high profits when he sells them. On the other hand if he believes that the price of tomatoes will be low he will produce fewer tomatoes, or perhaps none at all, and he may then devote his energies to the production of some other vegetable.

It is possible to obtain a supply schedule for each individual seller, which relates the price of the good and the quantity that the seller will be prepared to sell at each price. The individual supply schedules can be added together to obtain a market supply schedule. The supply schedule for tomatoes for the United Kingdom per month might be as follows, for example:

Price (pence)	Supply (kilos per month)
70	600,000
60	550,000
50	475,000
40	400,000
30	300,000
20	200,000
10	50,000

Table 20. A market supply schedule for tomatoes (kilos per month)

Market supply curve

Using the information provided by the market supply schedule it is possible to construct a market supply curve, which relates the price and the quantity that sellers are prepared to sell.

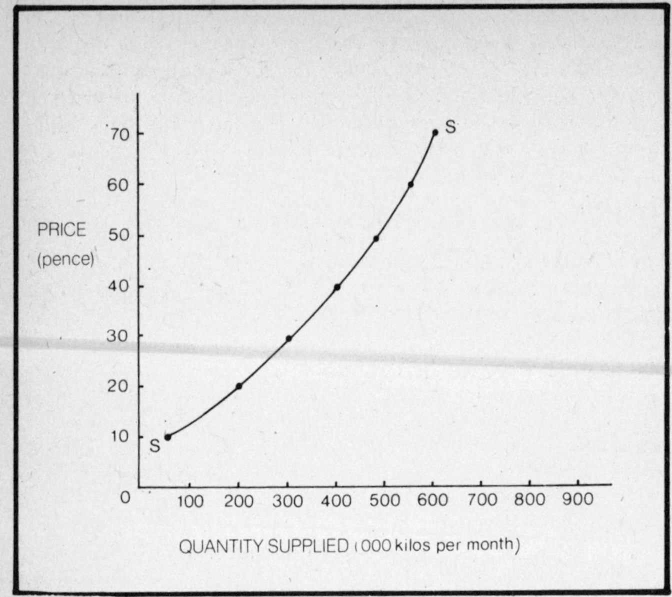

Figure 16. A market supply curve for tomatoes (kilos per month)

The conditions of supply

The underlying conditions of supply will determine the amount that sellers will be prepared to sell as well as the price of the product. It is important to distinguish between a change in the quantity that sellers are prepared to sell, and a change in supply. If the ruling price is 60p suppliers will be prepared to sell 550,000 kilos per month; if the price falls to 30p suppliers will only be prepared to sell 300,000 kilos per month. This increase in the quantity supplied is solely the effect of the change in price. If the conditions of supply change, however, a different quantity will be supplied at the same price.

The conditions of supply are:

1. Weather. The supply of many agricultural products is determined to a large extent by the weather. The supply curve will move to the left if poor weather conditions result in a bad harvest, whereas the supply curve will move to the right (indicating that more will be supplied at every price), if weather conditions have been favourable.

2. Technology. Improvements in technology reduce costs and encourage suppliers to supply greater quantities at each market price, thus shifting the supply curve to the right.

3. The cost of factors of production. A rise in the costs of suppliers caused by an increase in the prices of factors of production will cause the supply curve to move to the left, as suppliers will be prepared to supply a smaller quantity at each price. A reduction in the prices of these factors will move the supply curve to the right.

4. Taxes and subsidies. A tax on a good will have the same effect as an increase in the costs of production, and will thus shift the supply curve to the left by the amount of the tax. Thus if the sale of tomatoes is subject to a tax of 10p per kilo, and the current price is 40p, then suppliers will now only be prepared to supply the same quantity at a price of 50p. A subsidy will have the effect of shifting the supply curve to the right, since it will effectively reduce the costs of production.

5. The price of other goods. If the prices of other goods change, this may have an effect on the supply curve of the product in question. Most products are in competitive supply, that is, if a producer wishes to increase the supply of one good he can only do so by reducing his production of another good (assuming that the size of the firm remains constant). For example, if the price of lettuces rise and the price of tomatoes stays the same, the market gardener may decide to produce more lettuces and less tomatoes. Thus the increased output of one product has caused a smaller output for the other, and the goods are in competitive supply. This action will also shift the supply curve of tomatoes to the left. Some goods are in joint supply, for example if the price of wool rises the farmer will raise more sheep, but this will not only have the effect of increasing the output of wool, but it will also shift the supply of lamb to the right, even though its price has remained unchanged. Thus joint supply exists where the production of one good leads to the production of another good.
Changes in the conditions of supply will move the supply curve to the left or to the right. Table 21 gives the possible effects on the supply schedule of an increase in supply, and of a decrease in supply. Figure 17 illustrates these changes. The original supply curve is denoted by the letters SS; an increase in supply, causing a shift to the right is denoted by the letters S_1S_1, and a decrease in supply, causing a shift to the left is denoted by S_2S_2.

Price (pence)	Supply (a) An increase	(b) A decrease
70	850,000	375,000
60	800,000	325,000
50	725,000	250,000
40	650,000	175,000
30	550,000	75,000
20	450,000	0
10	300,000	0

Table 21. Schedules of (a) an increase in supply and (b) a decrease in supply.

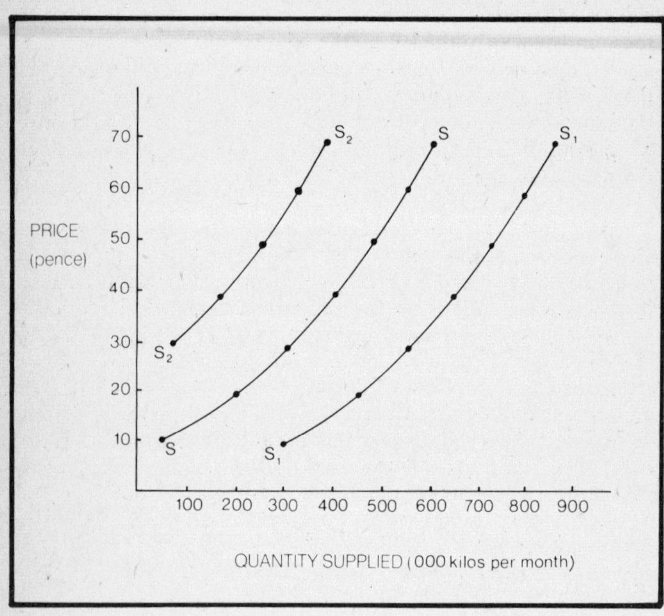

Figure 17. Changes in supply.

The determination of market price

The market price of a product is determined by the interaction of the forces of supply and demand. If the original demand schedule and supply schedule are examined side by side, as in Table 22, and the demand and supply curves DD and SS are illustrated on the same diagram, it can be seen that at only one price does supply equal demand, i.e. at a price of 40p the amount consumers wish to buy is 400,000 kilos per month, and the amount sellers wish to sell is 400,000 kilos per month; 40 pence is the market price for tomatoes, also called the equilibrium price. The equilibrium quantity is 400,000 kilos of tomatoes per month.

Price (pence)	Demand (kilos per month)	Supply (kilos per month)
70	100,000	600,000
60	150,000	550,000
50	250,000	475,000
40	400,000	400,000
30	550,000	300,000
20	700,000	200,000
10	900,000	50,000

Table 22. Demand and supply schedules for tomatoes.

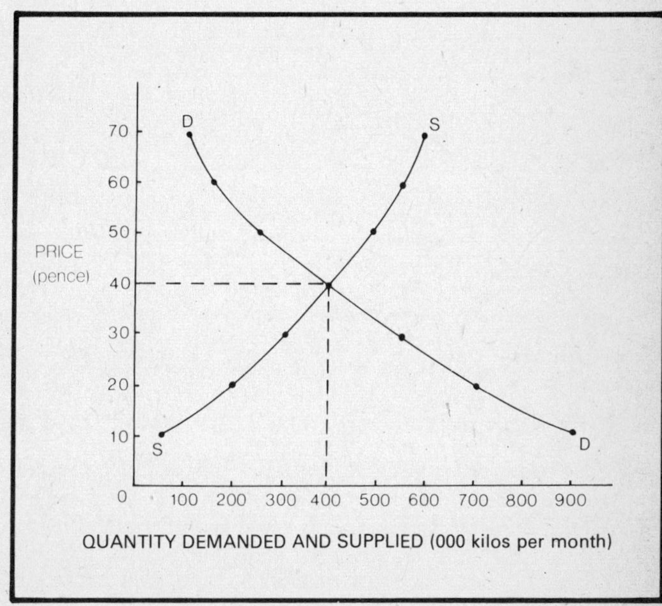

Figure 18. The determination of market price, the demand curve and the supply curve of tomatoes.

The market price will always move to the equilibrium position where demand and supply are equal.

If the market price is higher than the equilibrium price supply will exceed demand (e.g. if the price of tomatoes is 60p per kilo demand will be 150,000 kilos per month, but supply will be 550,000 kilos per month, and thus supply will exceed demand by 400,000 kilos per month). In this situation suppliers will be unable to sell all of their produce, and will have to lower their price. As price falls towards the equilibrium price buyers will buy more, and sellers will be prepared to sell less, until demand and supply are equal at the equilibrium price.

If the market price is lower than the equilibrium price demand will exceed supply (e.g. if the price of tomatoes is 20p per kilo demand for tomatoes will be 700,000 kilos per month, but supply will only be 200,000 kilos per month). As demand exceeds supply sellers will soon sell all of their output, and the price of the good will be forced up as buyers attempt to outbid each other to obtain the available quantities, and sellers see the opportunity to raise price. Once the price has risen to the equilibrium price demand will no longer exceed supply, and the price will remain stable.

The equilibrium price is so called because once the equilibrium price has been achieved, there is no tendency for price or quantity demanded and supplied to change, unless the conditions of demand or supply change.

Changes in price

The equilibrium price of a good or service can change if a change occurs in either the conditions of demand or the conditions of supply.

Figure 19, shows how a shift in the demand curve will cause both the equilibrium price and quantity to change. If demand increases the demand curve will shift to the right (supply will remain constant), as in Figure 19 where the demand curve shifts from DD to D_1D_1. This increase in demand will have the effect of increasing the equilibrium quantity, and raising equilibrium price. A decrease in demand, shifting the demand curve from DD to D_2D_2, will have the effect of lowering price and reducing the equilibrium quantity, as shown in Figure 19.

Changes in the conditions of supply can shift the supply curve to the left and the right, as was seen earlier in this chapter. An increase in supply (assuming demand to remain constant) is shown in Figure 20 where the supply curve shifts from SS to S_1S_1. This has the effect of decreasing price, and increasing the equilibrium quantity.

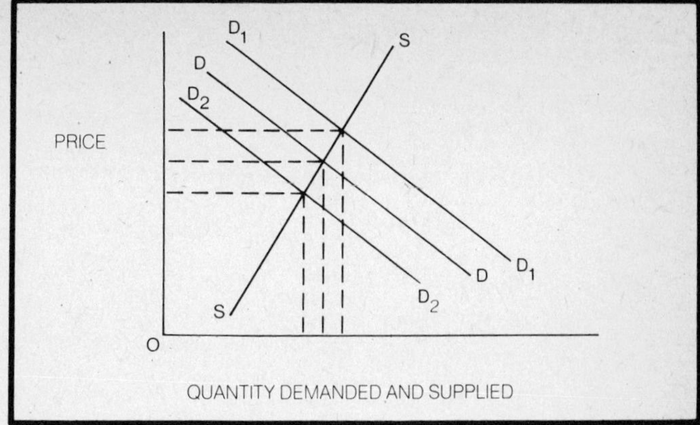

Figure 19. The effect on the market price of an increase in demand, and a decrease in demand.

A decrease in supply, shown in Figure 20, will cause the equilibrium price to rise and the equilibrium quantity to also fall.

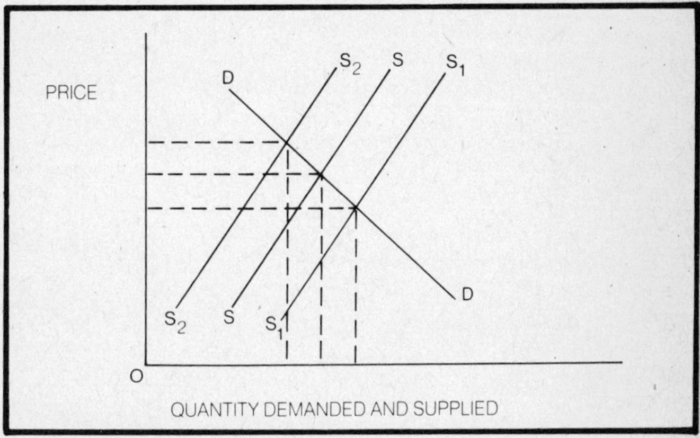

Figure 20. The effect on the market price of an increase in supply, and a decrease in supply.

Elasticity of demand

Elasticity of demand is the degree of responsiveness of the quantity demanded of a good to a change in its price. If the quantity demanded of a good is very responsive to a price change (that is, if a small change in price leads to a large change in the quantity demanded), then demand is said to be elastic.

If the quantity demanded of a good is relatively unresponsive to a change in price (that is, if even a large price change leads to only a small change in demand), then demand is said to be inelastic. Petrol and cigarettes are two goods which have an inelastic demand, for even large price increases only reduce demand by a small amount.

Elasticity of demand can be measured by using the following formula:

$$\text{Elasticity of demand} = \frac{\text{Proportionate change in quantity demanded}}{\text{Proportionate change in price}}$$

The demand schedule for tomatoes can be used to illustrate the calculation of the elasticity of demand.

Price	Demand
50p	250,000
40p	400,000

If the price rises by 10p from 40p to 50p per kilo, there has been a proportionate change in price of 10/40. Demand has fallen by 150,000 kilos, from 400,000 kilos to 250,000 kilos, so the proportionate change in quantity demanded is 150,000/400,000.

Thus the elasticity of demand for tomatoes at this particular point on the demand curve (from 40p per kilo to 50p per kilo) is

$$\frac{150{,}000}{400{,}000} \div \frac{10}{40} = 1\tfrac{1}{2}.$$

If the elasticity has a value of greater than 1, then demand is elastic at that price. If the elasticity of demand has a value of less than 1, demand is inelastic at that price. If the elasticity is 1, then demand at that price is unitary.

Elasticity of demand can vary between zero and infinity. A figure of zero indicates that the same quantity is demanded whatever the price, and this is illustrated in Figure 21(a). Infinite elasticity occurs when even a minute change in price causes an infinitely large change in the quantity demanded, this is illustrated in Figure 21(b). Where elasticity equals 1 the curve is a rectangular hyperbola and is illustrated in Figure 21(c).

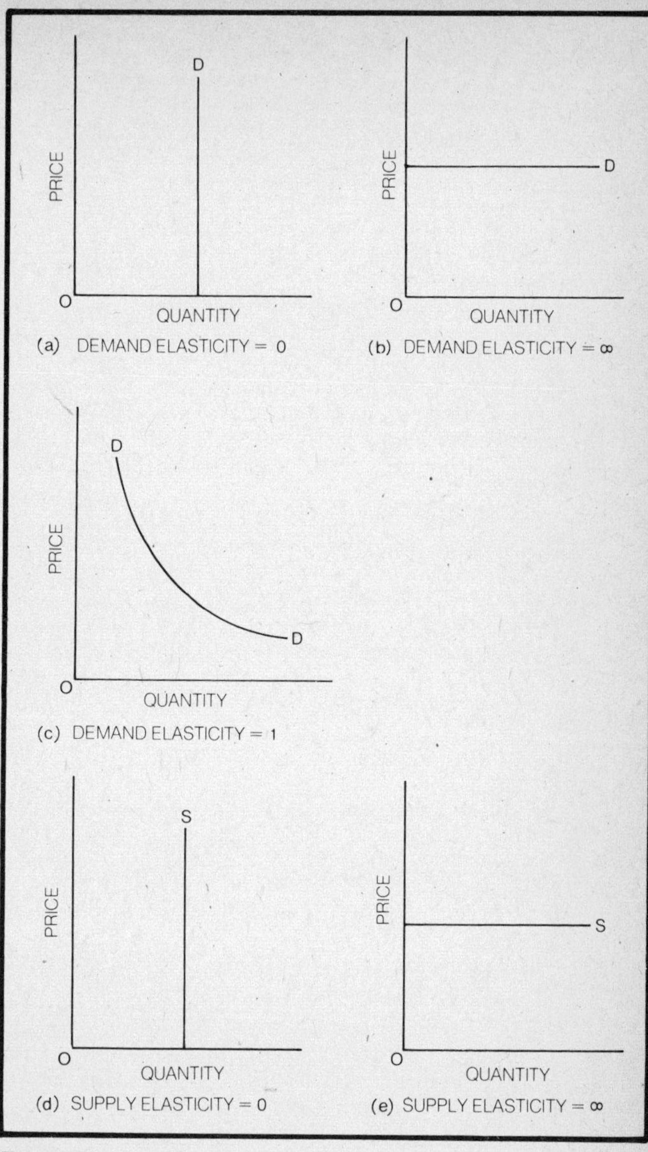

Figure 21. Elasticity of demand and elasticity of supply.

It should be stressed that all demand curves, except the three special cases illustrated, have a different elasticity at each point on the curve, and for this reason the figure obtained by the formula above gives a measure of point elasticity.

Factors determining the elasticity of demand

1. The availability of substitutes. This is the most important factor effecting the elasticity of demand. If a product has a close substitute at the prevailing market price it will tend to have an elastic demand, whereas if there is a lack of close substitutes demand will tend to be elastic.

2. The proportion of income spent on the good. If only a small proportion of income is spent on a good it will tend to have an inelastic demand, whereas if a high proportion of income is spent on it the demand will be elastic.

3. Habit forming goods. These tend to have an inelastic demand.

4. The variety of uses for a good. The more uses a good has the greater will be the tendency for its demand to be elastic, as there will be a large number of substitutes for it.

5. Luxuries and necessities. Some students wrongly believe that the necessities of life must have an inelastic demand, and those goods normally termed 'luxuries' have an elastic demand. This is not necessarily the case for two reasons. Firstly, problems arise in deciding which goods are necessities and which goods are luxuries. Secondly, luxury goods bought by the rich may well have an inelastic demand as they are capable of paying any new higher price.

Elasticity of supply

Elasticity of supply is a measure of the degree of responsiveness to changes in price. The formula for measuring supply elasticity is:

$$\text{Elasticity of supply} = \frac{\text{Proportionate change in quantity supplied}}{\text{Proportionate change in price}}$$

If elasticity of supply is greater than 1, then supply is elastic at that price. If elasticity of supply has a value of less than 1, supply is inelastic at that price. If the elasticity of supply has a value of 1, then supply has a unitary elasticity at that price.

Elasticity of supply can vary between zero and infinity. Figure 21(d) illustrates a perfectly inelastic supply curve, where elasticity equals zero, and where quantity supplied is unchanged by changes in price. Figure 21(e) illustrates a perfectly elastic supply curve, where elasticity equals infinity, in which case sellers are prepared to supply any amount at the price P.

Elasticity of supply is a more complex concept than the elasticity of demand. The major factors which determine the elasticity of supply are firstly, the ease and the cost of attracting the necessary extra factors of production in order to produce the extra supply. Secondly, elasticity of supply varies over time, in fact elasticity of supply tends to increase over time. For example, if the price of wheat increases, farmers will be unable to increase supply until the following year.

Key terms

A market is a place or an area where the buyers and sellers of a good or service are in contact with one another for the purpose of trading the product and fixing price.
Demand is the desire to purchase a good or service backed by the willingness and ability to pay for it.
The market demand curve shows the relationship between the price of a good and the quantity that consumers wish to purchase.
The conditions of demand are the prices of other goods, the real income of consumers, tastes and fashions, advertising, and population.
Supply is that quantity that sellers are prepared to sell at a given price.
The market supply curve shows the relationship between the price and the quantity that sellers are prepared to sell.
The conditions of supply are the weather, technology, the cost of factors of production, taxes and subsidies and the price of other goods.
Equilibrium price is that price at which the quantity that buyers wish to buy is equal to the quantity that sellers wish to sell.
Elasticity of demand is the responsiveness of demand to changes in price.
Elasticity of supply is the responsiveness of supply to changes in price.

Chapter 10
Competition and Monopoly

The successful working of the market economy in allocating resources is effected by the degree of competition between buyers and sellers, as this may effect the determination of market price. For example, if only one buyer exists for a certain product, then this buyer could 'play' supplying firms against one another in order to force down the market price below the equilibrium price. This would mean that the allocation of resources would not be determined by equilibrium price, but according to the degree of power enjoyed by the buyer. On the other hand, buyers might be faced with a single seller of a particular product, who might be able to force the price of the product higher than would have been the case if many suppliers competed to sell their own output. In this case the allocation of resources will be determined by the market power of the seller.

Economists have devised two limiting cases which describe the extreme conditions of market competition. At one end of the competitive spectrum is **perfect competition,** (perfect in the sense that competition between firms is of the highest degree possible), where there are many small buyers and sellers. At the opposite end is **monopoly,** where there is no competition at all, because there is only one seller. Both these situations are examined in detail below, although it is highly unlikely that either of them has ever existed in real life. Real-life markets lie between the two extremes, some approaching perfect competition and others tending to monopoly.

Perfect competition

Perfect competition is a market situation where the following conditions operate:

1. There is a large number of buyers.
2. There is a large number of sellers.
3. No buyer or seller is large enough to be able to effect the market price by their own action.
4. The product is homogenous (i.e. identical).
5. Perfect information is available between buyers and sellers, regarding prices offered and prices asked.
6. New sellers can enter the market to compete on the same basis as existing sellers.

7. Economic friction does not exist within the market. That is, goods and factors are occupationally and geographically mobile and transport costs are assumed to be nil.

From these assumptions it is possible to construct a graphical representation of the perfectly competitive model. Figure 22(a) shows how the market price (OP) is determined by the interaction of market supply (SS) and market demand (DD). Figure 22(b) illustrates a representative firm in the industry which faces a perfectly elastic demand curve indicating it can sell all that it wishes at the market price (OP). If the firm raises price above the market price it will sell nothing at all, whereas if it reduces price by a minute amount demand will increase infinitely. The price (OP) that the firm obtains for each unit it sells also represents the firm's average revenue (AR), or revenue per unit sold. Average revenue can be calculated by dividing total revenue (TR) by units sold. Marginal revenue (MR) is the extra revenue that the firm obtains by selling an extra unit. Under perfect competition the seller will only sell at the market price, and the marginal revenue will therefore equal the market price. Thus under perfect competition:

Price = Average revenue = Marginal revenue (P=AR=MR).

Any firm, regardless of the market conditions under which it operates, will continue to produce whilst the extra revenue received exceeds the extra cost of producing one extra unit.

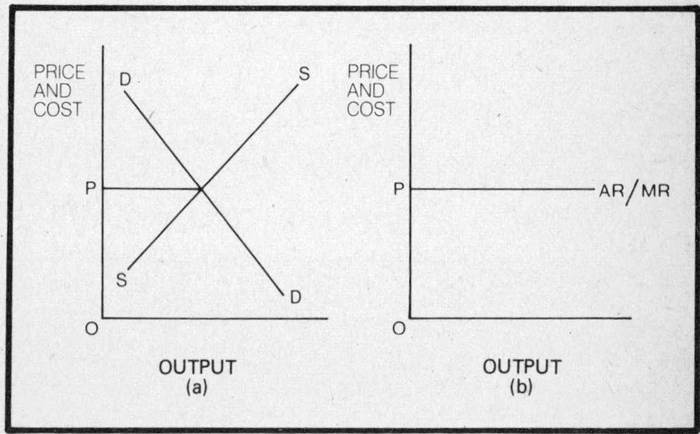

Figure 22. Perfect competition.

That is whilst MR is greater than MC. In fact, a firm will continue to sell right up to that point where MR=MC to obtain the maximum profit.

A firm under perfect competition faces fierce competition from its rivals, and it will therefore operate at that level of output where its average costs are lowest – at the optimum level of output. As was seen in Chapter 4, average costs are at a minimum where MC=AC.

Therefore, a firm operating under the conditions of perfect competition will produce at that level of output where:

P=AR=MR=MC=AC

and this is illustrated in Figure 23.

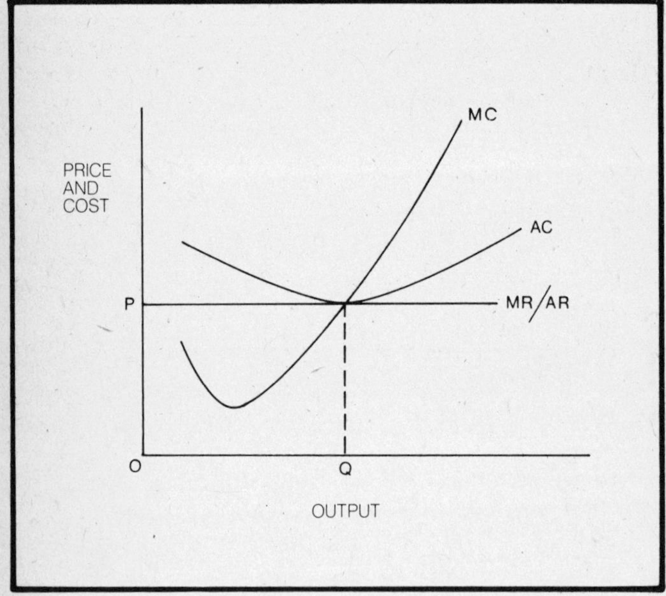

Figure 23. The output of the firm under perfect competition.

The firm will sell at the market price of OP a quantity of OQ. As AR=AC, the firm will be covering all its costs and will be earning normal profits.

Perfect competition, as a market form is claimed to have certain advantages. Firstly, as firms produce at the lowest point on the average cost curve, inefficient firms will be driven from the industry and economic resources will be used efficiently. Secondly, as there are many small sellers and buyers, consumers will benefit from low prices, and will not suffer at the hands of dealers who have excessive bargaining power.

Monopoly

Monopoly is a market situation where one firm or individual produces the entire output of a product. Although some of the assumptions which apply to perfect competition do not apply to monopoly, the monopolist differs from perfectly competitive firms in one essential aspect. If the monopolist wishes to sell more of its product then it must reduce price; if price is raised then the quantity sold will decrease. The monopolist has therefore some control over either the output or the price of the product, and is able to influence the market for its own gain.

The effects of monopoly

1. Monopoly results in a lower quantity being produced at a higher price, than would have been the case if the industry was competitive.
2. The monopolist does not produce at the optimum level of output and thus resources are not used efficiently.
3. The monopolist may become inefficient because there is no incentive to reduce costs (as there is with competition).

Beneficial effects of monopoly

There are certain circumstances in which a monopoly can be more efficient than a large number of small firms operating in a competitive manner. If the monopolist is able to take full advantage of large economies of scale, he will be able to produce at a lower average cost than smaller firms, although there is no guarantee that these cost advantages will be passed on to the consumer in the form of lower prices. Some goods and services require that production is carried on by a monopolist to avoid duplication, as is the case with the public utilities such as water, gas and electricity. These are called 'natural monopolies' and are usually operated by public enterprise.

Forms of monopoly

In theory, monopoly exists where a single firm supplies the total output of a product. In practice firms can enjoy monopoly profits even when there are several suppliers, if these firms choose to combine together and act as a single firm. Such practices by firms are called Restrictive practices, because they restrict competition, and at one time they were common in the United Kingdom. The main forms of monopoly are examined below:

1. **A single firm** may not produce the total output of a product, but its share of the market may be so large that it can act like a monopolist.

2. **Local monopolies** may exist for products which are expensive to transport; one firm may supply a particular area or region.

3. **Trade associations** are often formed by firms to represent their industry. However, in the past some trade associations have operated a wide range of restrictive practices designed to make high profits for member firms. Such practices have included price and output agreements, boycotts of other firms and collusive tendering.

4. **Cartels** are selling syndicates. Firms sell their output to the cartel; the cartel markets their output as a single output and distributes the profits amongst member firms. The government sponsors the Marketing Boards for agricultural produce, and these are cartels.

Monopoly policy in Britain

The government has attempted to control monopoly in the United Kingdom through legislation relating to the single firm monopoly, restrictive trade practices and mergers (which may of course lead to the formation of a single firm monopoly). Major anti-monopoly legislation is listed below.

The Monopolies and Restrictive Practices Act 1948 established a Monopolies Commission to investigate and report on monopoly situations where more than one third of a product's supply came from a firm or a group of firms acting together. The Commission found restrictive practices were widespread in British industry which led to legislation to combat such practices.

The Restrictive Trade Practices Act 1956 established a Registrar of Restrictive Trading Agreements with whom such practices had to be registered. The Restrictive Practices Court was set up to examine restrictive practices to decide whether they were in the public interest and ordered their cessation if they were not. Since the passing of the Act more than 3000 agreements have been registered, many of which have been abandoned, and only 11 of which have been upheld as being in the public interest.

The Resale Prices Act 1964 abolished the fixing of the selling price in retail outlets by manufacturers. Few firms appealed and even fewer have been allowed to continue this practice.

The Monopolies and Mergers Act 1965 provided the power to refer any mergers to the Monopolies and Mergers Commission which created or intensified a monopoly situation, or if the gross assets taken over exceeded £5 million.

The Fair Trading Act 1973 is built upon previous legislation, and contains almost all current legislation on monopoly, mergers and restrictive practices. A Director General of Fair Trading was appointed to take over the powers of the Registrar of Restrictive Trading Agreements and some amendments were made to restrictive practice legislation. The market share criterion for monopoly was reduced from a third to a quarter and the Act investigates export monopolies and local monopolies.

The Restrictive Trade Practices Act 1976 requires the registration of agreements over virtually the whole range of commercial activities. Prior to this Act certain practices had been outside the scope of legislation.

The Competition Act 1980 enables the Director General of Fair Trading to investigate any business practice (whether in the public or private sector) which may restrict, distort or prevent competition in the production, supply or acquisition of goods or service in Britain. If a practice is found to be anti-competitive, the Director General can refer it to the Monopolies and Mergers Commission to establish whether it operates against the public interest and, if necessary, the Secretary of State has powers to take remedial action.

The Competition Act also empowers the Secretary of State to refer to the Monopolies and Mergers Commission any question on the efficiency and costs of, the service provided by, or the possible abuse of a monopoly situation by, particular named bodies in the public sector.

Key terms

Perfect competition is a market form where competition is at the highest degree possible.

Monopoly is where the output of a product is in the hands of a single supplier.

Restrictive practices are agreements made between firms which restrict competition.

Chapter 11
Wages and Trade Unions

Wages

A wage may be defined as a payment, made under contract by an employer for the services of labour. The economist includes all payments for the services of labour under the heading, wages, including salaries, fringe benefits, bonus payments and payments received through profit sharing agreements.

Methods of payment

Employees may receive payment from their employers in a variety of ways. Blue collar workers usually receive a weekly wage paid in cash whereas white collar workers are more likely to receive a monthly salary paid into their bank account by cheque. About three-quarters of wage earners in the U.K. are paid on a time-rate basis, where their earnings are determined by the number of hours worked each week. The remaining one-quarter of wage earners are paid on a piece-rate basis, and their earnings are dependent on the quantity of their output. Many employees also receive fringe benefits, which are payments in the form of goods and services such as luncheon vouchers to a secretary, free coal to a coalminer and a firm's car to a sales representative. In recent years some firms have introduced profit sharing schemes for employees. It is quite common for an employee to receive payment by a combination of two or more of these methods, each of which is examined in greater detail below.

Time rates

The majority of blue collar workers are paid on an hourly basis, they 'clock on' when starting work and 'clock off' at the end of their day. Their wages are calculated on the number of hours at work. These workers usually work a specified number of hours per week, e.g. 40, and they may have the opportunity to work 'overtime' if they wish. Overtime is usually paid at a higher rate of pay. Some white collar workers are also paid on an hourly basis and can obtain overtime payments for extra hours worked. Time rates have the advantage that workers can concentrate on producing a high quality output, but they do have the disadvantage that as both poor and good workers receive the same payments there is little incentive for employees to work hard. Management may need to employ supervisory staff to ensure that workers produce an output of an adequate quality and quantity.

For some types of work time rates are the only feasible method of payment. When output cannot easily be measured as in police work or nursing, or when a high rate of output may be harmful or impossible, such as driving a bus, time rates must be used.

Some workers are paid on a salary system. This is one in which a fixed amount is paid each year in monthly instalments; salary earners do not usually receive payments for overtime. A salary system can be used when the employment itself provides an incentive to work hard, and where workers receive a high level of job satisfaction, such as in the professions. Salaried workers are often graded on the basis of their experience and qualifications and receive payments accordingly.

Piece rates

A piece-rate system of payment is one whereby a worker is paid according to his output, and thus a fast worker will earn more than a slow one.

The major advantages of this type of system is that workers are encouraged to work hard to obtain a high income, and good workers are rewarded for their efforts. Workers are encouraged to suggest methods of raising output, and supervision to ensure that workers actually work is unnecessary. Furthermore, capital becomes more intensely used and this reduces capital costs per unit.

However the piece-rate system has several disadvantages. Workers are encouraged to rush and may produce shoddy work, thus although supervisors are unnecessary firms often have to employ staff to check that output reaches a minimum standard of quality. Secondly workers may 'overwork' in their attempts to earn high wages, resulting in poor health, a high labour turnover and a poor quality output. The operation of piece-rate systems have, in the past been accused of causing discontent amongst workers and also between workers and management resulting in poor industrial relations and conflict. Some firms have successfully introduced schemes in which workers are organized into groups, and bonus rewards are made on a group basis.

Fringe benefits

Fringe benefits have formed an increasing part of total earnings in recent years. Policies to control increases in wages have encouraged employees to attempt to obtain non-wage benefits. Fringe benefits take various forms, and the most common include luncheon vouchers, cheap mortgage facilities, expense accounts, company cars, medical insurance, pension schemes and cheap travel facilities. In the past only white collar workers tended to obtain fringe benefits, but it is becoming increasingly common for blue collar workers to demand and to be offered benefits of this type.

Profit sharing

Some firms have introduced profit sharing schemes for their employees, of which there are two basic types. In the first scheme the firm shares a proportion of its profits amongst its workers in the form of a bonus payment. In the second scheme, workers are either given, or are able to buy cheaply, shares in the company which entitle them to a dividend financed from the firm's profits. The supporters of profit sharing claim that it encourages loyalty and effort, as well as reducing industrial conflict as workers have a financial stake in their firm. However, if the firm fares badly workers may suffer if the profits they receive form a sizeable share of their income. In the collapse of Rolls Royce in 1971, some workers lost not only their jobs, but all their savings which they had invested in the company.

For these reasons many trade unions are highly suspicious of profit sharing schemes.

Many employees will receive payment using a combination of these methods. For example, a coalminer might receive a basic wage dependent upon the hours he has worked, a bonus payment dependent upon the productivity of the colliery where he works, and fringe benefits in the form of free coal and the provision of a sports and social club.

Wage rates and average earnings

It is important to distinguish between the basic wage rate and average earnings. The hourly or weekly wage rate in a particular occupation for a specified length of working week (normally 40 hours) which is set by national wage agreements is called the basic wage rate. However, average weekly earnings are often higher than the basic wage rate as many employees receive overtime payments, bonuses, shift-work allowances, piece rate payments and various other additions. Average earnings are total earnings before the deduction of tax, national insurance and pension contributions. Wage rates and average earnings differ substantially, and this difference is termed wage drift. When wage rates are held down, workers will attempt to work longer hours and will try to increase their bonus payments, and in this way average earnings can rise much faster than wage rates. When basic wage rates are rising quickly, workers might reduce overtime working, and thus wage rates will increase faster than average earnings, and this will reduce wage drift.

Wage differences

	Average gross weekly earnings			
	April 1976		April 1970	
Occupation	£	position	£	position
Academics	107·1	1	44·2	2
Professional engineers	98·5	2	38·6	3
Managers	97·3	3	53·1	1
Teachers	90·3	4	35·9	4
Coalminers	80·7	5	25·4	13
Policemen	78·5	6	29·4	7
Train drivers	74·5	7	28·9	8
Welders	74·1	8	31·3	5
Fitters	72·9	9	30·4	6
Bus drivers	71·6	10	26·3	11
HGV drivers	67·5	11	27·2	9
Postmen	67·4	12	25·5	12
Motor mechanics	61·5	13	26·6	10
General labourers	56·3	14	22·0	14
Farm workers	46·8	15	17·6	15

Table 23. Average gross weekly earnings of selected occupations.

The table above gives a breakdown of average earnings, and the differences in earnings between some of the major occupations of the United Kingdom. There are many factors which determine the relative position in the table of a particular occupation. Specifically differences between occupational earnings exist for the following reasons:

Skill. Skilled men are likely to earn more than unskilled men, partly because their output has a higher value, and partly because a higher wage will be needed to compensate for periods of education and training which may involve a loss in potential earnings. Thus doctors can be expected to earn more than nurses, accountants can be expected to earn more than their clerks. Table 24 illustrates the relationship between earnings and skills in engineering and shipbuilding.

	Industry	
	Engineering	Shipbuilding
Skilled workers	£66·28	£75·38
Labourers	£52·23	£63·23

Table 24. Average weekly earnings (1976).

Dangerous and dirty jobs. Higher wages will have to compensate individuals entering occupations which are dangerous or dirty. Examples include coalminers, firemen, steeplejacks and furnacemen.
Responsibility. Higher wages can be expected to accompany the degree of responsibility involved in an occupation. For example, lorry drivers are paid in relation to the size of their vehicle.
Security of employment. Some occupations involve long periods of unemployment or short-time working, as is found in the building trade during the winter months. Some jobs, such as professional sport, have a relatively short working life. The greater the insecurity of employment, the higher wages will have to be to attract workers into that line of employment.
Trade unions. Wages are normally better in those occupations where union membership is high, and where a trade union can present a united front to management.
Other factors. Wage differences will also be caused by an occupation's social status – jobs which have a low social status may require a higher wage to attract labour. Higher wages may also be necessary for boring work, as individuals can be expected to accept a lower wage for a more interesting job.

Differences in wages give rise to the terms differentials and relativities. Both these terms refer to the relative wage rates earned by different groups of workers. For example, if labourers in a certain industry received a higher wage rise than skilled workers then the differential between the groups would have been reduced. Relativity refers to the relative position of a particular occupation. For example, according to Table 23, the relative position of coalminers improved substantially between 1970 and 1976.

Equal pay

The Equal Pay Act of 1970, which came into force in December 1975 attempts to eliminate discrimination between men and women with regard to pay and working conditions. This Act states that a woman must not be paid less than a man when she is employed on work of the same or broadly similar nature. The Sex Discrimination Act of 1975 makes it unlawful for an employer to discriminate against a man or a woman on the grounds of sex, in respect of recruitment, promotion, benefits, dismissals and training.

In the past wage differences between the sexes were considerable, and frequently different pay scales existed for men and women doing the same job. There has been a reduction in this differential during the 1970s reflecting the effects of legislation and the changing status of women in society.

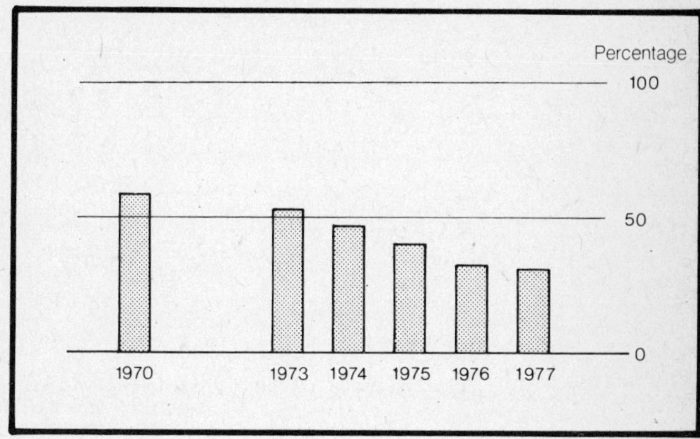

Figure 24. Percentage by which the average hourly earnings of men exceeded those of women, 1970 to 1977.

The major reason for the continued difference in the average wage rates, despite the equal pay legislation is that women tend to be found working in low paid jobs, such as catering. A further factor is that far fewer women are members of trade unions. Only about 40% of female employees are members of trade unions, the corresponding figure for male employees is 60%.

The average earnings of women are much lower than those of men, and the major reason for this is that men work more overtime. In retailing and banking women's earnings are well below those of their male colleagues. Even in teaching, which has a strict equal pay system, women earn 20% less than men.

Trade unions

At the end of 1979 there were 477 listed trade unions in the United Kingdom. They had a combined membership of 13·2 million from the 21·7 employees in employment. About 80 per cent of trade union members were in the largest 25 unions, each having over 100,000 members. The largest nine trade unions and their membership at the end of 1977 are given below.

Union	Membership (000s)
Transport and General Workers Union (TGWU)	1,856
Amalgamated Union of Engineering Workers (AUEW)	1,428
National Union of General and Municipal Workers (NUGMW)	881
National Association of Local Government Officers (NALGO)	753
National Union of Public Employees (NUPE)	691
Association of Scientific, Technical and Managerial Staff (ASTMS)	491
Union of Shop, Distributive and Allied Workers (USDAW)	470
Electrical, Electronic, Plumbing and Telecommunications Union (EEPTU)	420
Union of Construction, Allied Trades and Technicians (UCATT)	347

Table 25. Membership of the largest 9 unions in the U.K. (1979)

There are four basic types of trade union in the United Kingdom.

1. Craft unions

Most craft unions were formed during the nineteenth century to organize groups of skilled workers within a particular trade or craft, such as engineers or carpenters. Craft unions continue to attract skilled workers who may feel that they have more in common with workers of the same skill, rather than other workers in the same factory. There are two problems associated with craft unions; firstly, wage bargaining becomes complicated when many small unions representing groups of skilled workers are involved; secondly, inter-union disputes concerning relative wage levels, and 'demarcation' disputes over the allocation of work between groups of workers, are much more likely to occur. These problems weaken the trade union movement as a whole, and weaken the unions' bargaining position with management, who are able to play on inter-union rivalry. The major craft unions in Britain are the AUEW and the EEPTU.

2. General unions

Many general unions were formed during the late nineteenth century to organize the semi-skilled and unskilled workers, who could not join the craft unions. General unions do not confine themselves to one craft or industry and are able to recruit large numbers of workers from wide areas of industry; the sheer volume of members can make such unions very powerful. However, the large number of different groups within such unions can be a source of weakness if some workers pursue sectional interests, or if a conflict arises between different groups of workers within the union. The major general unions are the TGWU and the GMWU.

3. Industrial unions

Industrial unions attempt to organize the workers in one industry into a single body. This type of union is common in the United States and West Germany, and has several advantages. Collective bargaining is simplified as management has a single union to negotiate with. Furthermore, inter-union and demarcation disputes are unlikely to occur, and workers can present a united front to management. The major problem experienced by these unions is that some workers feel that their sectional interests may be submerged within the union, and this may cause disputes within the union, or may discourage workers from joining an industrial union. For example, although the National Union of Railwaymen has sought to represent all railway workers, many drivers are members of the craft-based union ASLEF.

4. White collar unions

The first white collar unions were formed at the turn of the century, as employment expanded in the white collar occupations such as teaching, shop work and office work. Traditionally, many white collar workers shunned union membership as they considered that they had more in common with management than the blue collar union members. Added to this, the better pay and working conditions of the white collar workers reduced the need for union representation.

Today, however, the white collar unions represent the fastest growing sector within the trade union movement. The improvements in pay and working conditions which have been obtained by the white collar unions, together with the growing insecurity of employment in these occupations, have encouraged many white collar workers to become union members. The largest white collar unions are NALGO, ASTMS and NUT. As an illustration of the rate of growth in white collar unionism, ASTMS increased its membership from 351,000 to 491,000 between 1974 and 1979, an increase of almost 10 per cent each year.

Union organization

Although internal union organization varies from union to union, certain common characteristics do exist in their administrative structures. The following description could broadly apply to most unions.

Members of a union from within a small geographical area form the local unit of the union – the branch. **The branch** is likely to include workers from several different factories, although very large factories may contain sufficient union members to form a branch. The branches of some unions are based on an individual workplace; in the National Union of Mineworkers, for example, the branch is based on individual collieries. Branch meetings elect delegates to the national conference of the union and discuss local issues. In the larger unions branches also send delegates to regional or area committees, which are groups of branches.

The yearly **annual conference** is the policy making body of the union, and its decisions determine the path that a union follows. The day to day running of the union is the responsibility of the **National Executive,** which meets regularly. In some unions the members of the National Executive are elected by the annual conference, in others they are elected by a national ballot or a local ballot if the executive member is to specifically represent an area. Many unions use a combination of the two methods, electing the most senior officers by ballot. The most important member of the National Executive is the **General Secretary** or **President** of the union. The General Secretary and other members of the National Executive are normally responsible for national negotiations with employers. They also represent the views and interests of their members to the government and other organizations.

Local bargaining

Formal bargaining at a national level relating to wages and conditions takes place between the leaders of unions and employers. However, local conditions may vary considerably from area to area and from factory to factory, and thus there is scope for local bargaining to take place between management and workers.

Union members usually elect one of their number to act as their spokesman and he is called the 'shop steward'; he is an ordinary workman and will carry out his duties both during his own time and during normal working hours, as many employers allow shop stewards a specified number of hours each week to perform their duties. It is common for all the shop stewards from one factory to have regular meetings, even though they may represent workers from different unions, and they usually elect a chairman or convenor as he is also known, who can then act as the representative of all the union members in a particular factory. Factory negotiations between shop stewards and managers deal with such issues as the level of bonus payments, the length and timing of breaks, job allocation and other working practices. Workers often attach more importance to local plant bargaining then to national agreements.

The aims of trade unions

The Trades Union Congress (TUC) has distinguished ten main objectives of trade unions. They are:

1. Improved terms of employment.
2. Improved physical environment at work.
3. Full employment and national prosperity.
4. Security of employment and income.
5. Improved social security schemes.
6. Fair shares in national income and wealth.
7. Industrial democracy.
8. A voice in government.
9. Improved public and social services.
10. Public control and planning of industry.

The functions of trade unions

Trade unions attempt to achieve their aims in three ways: Firstly, they engage in direct consultation with management to attempt to improve the wages and conditions of work of their members. Secondly, they act as a pressure group on government, and try to persuade governments of all political parties to pass legislation, and carry out general economic policies which will benefit their members. Thirdly, they provide certain direct benefits for their members, such as unemployment benefit. All these are discussed in more detail below.

1. Collective bargaining. About three-quarters of employees in the United Kingdom are covered by agreements made between the representatives of workers and employers; the representatives of workers are invariably trade unions. Collective agreements normally cover two areas, firstly they specify the basic rates of pay, hours worked and holidays; secondly, they specify the procedure to be followed to reach agreements, and the procedure to be followed in the case of dispute. The normal procedure is that a union will present its case for improvements in pay and conditions which will include specific proposals. The employers will consider the union's case and make an offer. The offer may be accepted or rejected, if rejected more talks will follow until the two sides come to an agreement. Occasionally, the two sides fail to reach agreement. In this situation the independent Advisory, Conciliation and Arbitration Service may offer conciliation. ACAS assistance is sought in 2,000–3,000 disputes each year and about 80% of them are resolved in a manner acceptable to both parties. When agreement cannot be made through this method, the two parties can refer the claim to arbitration; an arbitrator will be appointed who will prepare a report and award. Although the award is not legally binding it is usual for the two sides to accept the claim. Annually, 300–400 requests are made for arbitration. The two sides may still fail to agree, or may have been unwilling to use ACAS, and in such cases an industrial dispute may occur. Industrial disputes are examined later in this chapter.

2. Influencing government policy. Trade unions attempt to influence government policy in two areas. Firstly, they press for specific items of legislation which will improve the working conditions, terms of employment, social security benefits and the status of their members. Examples of legislation supported by trade unions for these reasons include the Trade Union and Labour Relations Acts of 1974 and 1976, the Employment Protection Act of 1975 and the Health and Safety at Work Act of 1974. Secondly, trade unions support, and ask for a general economic strategy which will further the interests of the trade union movement as a whole. Trade unions are likely to support the economic policies associated with the Labour Party.

3. Provision of benefits. The benefits available to union members vary considerably from union to union. Some unions provide benefits in case of illness, accident, death and retirement, others do not even pay a disputes benefit when their members are on official strike. On average unions pay out about 30% of the contributions they receive on benefits.

Industrial action

Industrial action is used by workers to put pressure on employers when collective bargaining has been unsuccessful. The forms of action which workers can take, together with the incidence of disputes in the United Kingdom in recent years is given below.

Strikes. A strike is a complete withdrawal of labour by workers. Official strikes are supported by the relevant trade union, and strikers will normally receive strike pay. Unofficial strikes do not have the backing of the union. Official strikes tend to be fewer in number, but last much longer than unofficial strikes, which are often resolved in a short period of time. The large majority of strikes are wage disputes, as can be seen from Figure 25, which shows the number of working days lost through strikes from 1957 to 1977.

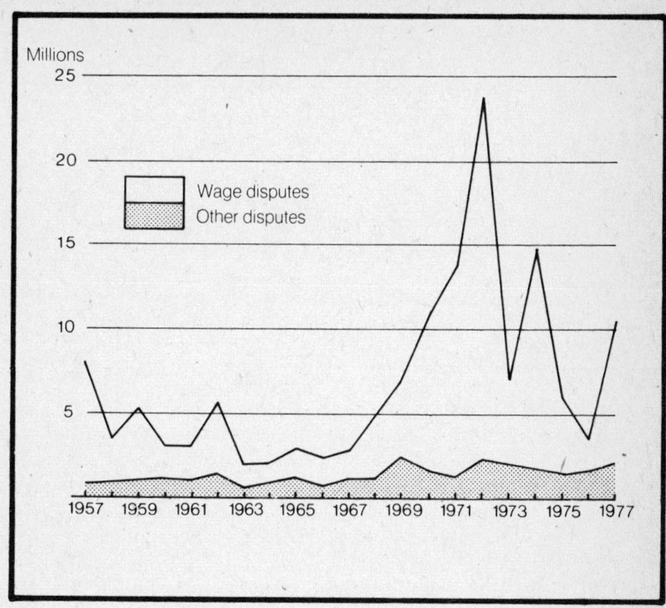

Figure 25. Working days lost through industrial disputes 1957–1977.

The incidence of strikes in the U.K. is often exaggerated. The number of days lost even during the early 1970s (in 1972 22 million working days), was quite small in relation to the 330 million days lost through illness for which sickness benefit was paid, and as sickness benefit is not paid for short absences, the true number of days lost through sickness must have been far higher. Neither is the U.K. one of the most strike-prone nations. Figures published by the International Labour Office for the years 1967 to 1976 showed the U.K. to have fewer days lost per thousand employees than Australia, the United States, Italy and Canada. Britain does however, lose more days than West Germany, France, Japan and Sweden.

Strikes are often accompanied by **picketing,** which is an attempt by strikers to persuade others at the factory to support them, either by joining the dispute or by refusing to do the work of workers on strike. Peaceful picketing is allowed by law.

Overtime ban. This form of action can be highly effective in those industries where staff shortages exist, and workers are normally relied upon to work overtime.

Work to rule. In some industries there are a large number of regulations which are usually ignored to ensure the smooth running of the firm. In these situations workers rigidly stick to all the regulations with the result that the organization may be brought to a halt in a very short time.

A 'go-slow' occurs when workers carry out their duties at a slower rate than normal. Like the work to rule this can bring an organization to a standstill.

Sympathy action. Sometimes, other groups of workers support unionists taking strike action, either by striking themselves, or by refusing to deliver goods to the strike-bound factory, or may refuse to work on the products of the firm.

The Trades Union Congress

The Trades Union Congress was formed in 1868, and represents the views and interests of the 109 trade unions which are affiliated to it, and which in 1981 had a combined membership of 12·1 million. Delegates from the affiliated trade unions attend the annual TUC conference to formulate TUC policy and elect the 38 members of the General Council, who are responsible for the running of the Congress and who take most of the main decisions on the basis of the views expressed, through the votes cast, by the affiliated unions at the conference. Members of the General Council sit on several government committees, including the National Economic Development Council (NEDC). The TUC's main power lies in its ability, as a pressure group, to represent the views of the twelve million trade unionists who are members of affiliated unions. The TUC's power is often exaggerated, and contrary to widespread belief it cannot call, nor can it halt any form of industrial action, including a strike. Affiliated unions are autonomous bodies, and although the TUC can offer advice, unions have the right to reject it. A union can be investigated, and may be expelled from the TUC if its conduct is detrimental to the interests of the trade union movement.

The TUC can interfere in unofficial strikes by making recommendations to the union and employer concerned. In such cases affiliated trade unions are expected to comply with the TUC's recommendations.

The major criticisms of the TUC have been that on the one hand it is too powerful, and has too great an influence on government policy, and that it is not powerful enough because it has such little control over the affiliated unions, unlike comparable organizations in Sweden and West Germany.

Key terms

A wage is a payment for the services of labour.
A **fringe benefit** is a payment in the form of goods and/or services.
Time rates involve payment according to the number of hours worked.
Piece rates involve payment according to the quantity of work produced.
Wage drift refers to the difference between wage rates and average earnings.
A **differential** is the difference between the earnings of different groups of workers.
Collective bargaining is the process whereby representatives of employers and employees make collective agreements on wages and the conditions of work.
Industrial action is used by workers to put pressure on employers. The most common forms of action are the strike, the overtime ban, the work to rule and the 'go-slow'.
The **TUC** is an affiliation of 109 trade unions, with a combined membership of over twelve million, which represents the views and interests of its member unions.

Chapter 12
Money

Money can be defined as anything which can be used as a medium of exchange or as a measure of value and which is generally acceptable as such.

Barter

In a simple economy with a very basic division of labour it is possible for trade to be carried out by means of barter, i.e. the direct exchange (swop) of goods and services. For example, a fisherman who requires a quantity of wood can trade with a wood-cutter who has some wood to spare and requires fish. However, barter presents some difficulties:

1. It is necessary to find someone who has the required commodity and who is prepared to trade it for the commodity which is being offered, e.g. the fisherman may be unable to find a woodcutter who is prepared to trade with him.
2. There is some scope for argument concerning the rate of exchange, e.g. how many fish exchange for a bag of sticks?
3. A person may be unable to trade one large indivisible good for several small ones. Imagine the problem of exchanging an elephant for some wood, fish and clothing.
4. It is difficult to share in the output of a commodity. Picture a car worker receiving wages in steering wheels.

The functions of money

The limitations imposed by barter make such a system unsuitable for an economy using the division of labour. It is useful to examine the functions of money before discussing the development of money through the ages. The functions of money include:

1. Money serves as a medium of exchange and this enables the extension of the division of labour. The car worker does not receive his wages in steering wheels, but in money which he can then exchange for many other goods and services such as food, clothing or a visit to the cinema.
2. Money serves as a unit of account. There is no need to bargain about the rate of exchange as the price of a commodity is its value in money. This enables the comparison of goods and services indirectly through money. If a hamburger is 40p and a visit to the

cinema is 80p, then 2 hamburgers equal one visit to the cinema.
3. Money serves as a store of value. It is possible to save money to buy an expensive good. Storing other commodities might be difficult or expensive, e.g. livestock would have to be fed, perishables would soon deteriorate. The main disadvantage of holding money as a store of value is during periods of inflation when the exchange value of money declines.
4. Money serves as a means of making deferred payments. In a society without money, payments by instalment, or deferred payment is very difficult, and these are both important facets of a modern economy.

The functions which money performs has several advantages over a barter system:
1. Money encourages the division of labour, which can increase output per head and thus the standard of living.
2. Money makes loans and savings easier.
3. Money gives a person the ability to obtain the maximum satisfaction from his income as he can divide up his resources and wants into very small units.
4. Money is a highly liquid asset, and the holder can buy a commodity without having to worry about trying to find someone who will carry out an exchange of goods.
5. Money is easy to store.

The development of money

The limitations imposed by barter encouraged the use of goods which could be used as a medium of exchange. Sugar was used in the West Indies; elephants in Sri Lanka; other forms of 'money' included cocoa beans, fur pelts, salt, cattle, corn and olive oil. Such goods usually had some intrinsic value. The major problems with these early forms of money were that they varied in quality, were sometimes bulky and not easily divisible and were subject to deterioration.
These difficulties brought about the use of precious metals like gold and silver as money, and this brought several advantages; they were intrinsically valuable, they were easy to store and did not deteriorate over time, they were portable and although they were limited in supply there was enough to go around.

Paper money

During the sixteenth century, the wealthy began to deposit their gold in the vaults of goldsmiths, where it was more secure. In return the goldsmiths issued a note promising to pay the bearer a certain quantity of gold. The owners could either use the note to redeem the gold or to purchase goods and services, thus transferring the ownership of the deposits. After a time the goldsmiths began to issue the notes in convenient denominations such as £1 and £5. Soon the notes themselves began to be used as money and the individual could continue to redeem a quantity of gold with the promisory note; this fact ensured that the notes were generally acceptable as a payment for goods and services. With the passing of time, and the general acceptance of notes, the banks joined the goldsmiths and began to issue notes. It soon became clear that only a small fraction of the bank notes were presented for repayment in gold. This meant that the large part of the holdings of gold was left lying in the vaults. The bankers realised that they could issue notes with a total face value greatly in excess of the value of their holdings of gold, and still have enough gold to satisfy those who required repayment in gold. The banks were able to 'create money', because only a fraction of their note issue was backed by gold, i.e. they were engaged in 'fractional backing'. This was a highly profitable business as the money created in this way could be loaned at interest.

A series of crises in the eighteenth century during which note issuing organizations were unable to meet the demands for gold forced the government to control the issuing of notes through the Bank Charter Act of 1844. Since 1921 only The Bank of England has had the power to issue notes in England and Wales. The fractional backing of notes is now commonplace throughout the world and since 1931 it has not been possible to convert bank notes into gold in the U.K.

Notes and coins are generally acceptable as money and are able to perform the functions specified earlier in the chapter. Furthermore they are 'legal tender', which means that a creditor must by law accept them if they are offered in payment.

Bank deposits

In Britain today, only about 10% of the value of money transactions are settled by cash (notes and coins). The remaining 90% is settled by **cheque,** and any examination of money must include a consideration of the cheque as a means of payment. A cheque is a written instruction to a bank to pay a specified amount of money to a person or organization named, from the bank deposit of the drawer. The banks usually transfer the quantity of money from the bank account of the drawer into the bank account of the person named on the cheque. No money need change hands, the deposits of the drawer will be reduced by the amount of the cheque, and the deposits of the person named on the cheque will be increased by the same amount. Bank deposits are therefore money, in that they fulfil the functions of money listed earlier. Although the cheque is not legal tender, it is generally acceptable as a means of payment. The cheque has two distinct advantages in the settling of debts, they are convenient to hold and they do not require the expense and effort needed to transfer large quantities of cash.

Key terms

Money is anything which can be used as a medium of exchange or as a measure of value and which is generally acceptable as such.
Barter is the direct exchange of goods and services.
Fractional backing occurs when only a fraction of the note issue is backed by gold and precious metals.
A cheque is a written instruction to pay a specified amount to a person or organization named.

Chapter 13
Inflation

An inflation is an increase in the general level of prices, which results in a fall in the purchasing power of a given sum of money. Throughout the world inflation has been higher during the 1970s than during any other decade of the twentieth century. Table 26 illustrates this point.

	1960–1972	1973–1978
United Kingdom	3·8%	15·0%
All OECD countries*	3·5%	10·1%

Table 26. Annual rise in retail prices in the U.K. and all OECD countries 1960 to 1978.

* OECD refers to The Organisation for Economic Development which is a club of 24 industrial nations.

Inflation is regarded as one of the major economic problems facing Britain, and the control of inflation has been considered to be a main priority of government since the early 1970s. Table 27 and Figure 26, below show the extent of the inflation problem in the U.K. during recent years.

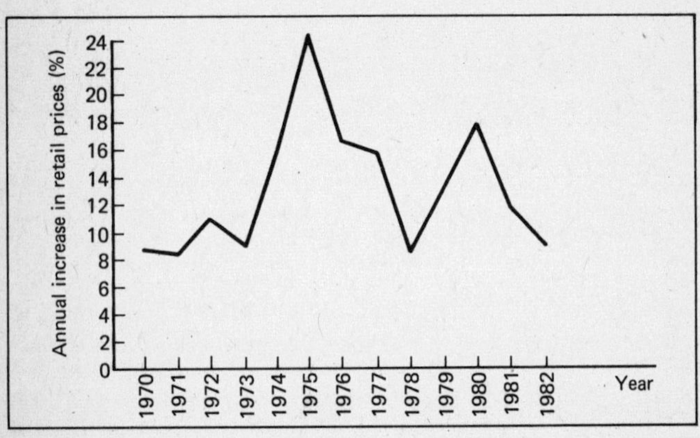

Figure 26. Average annual change in retail prices in the U.K. 1970 to 1981.

Year	Increase in retail prices (%)
1970	8·5
1971	8·2
1972	10·8
1973	9·2
1974	16·0
1975	24·2
1976	16·5
1977	15·9
1978	8·3
1979	13·4
1980	18·0
1981	11·9
1982 (projected)	9·5

Table 27. Average annual change in retail prices in the U.K. 1970 to 1982.

Measuring inflation

The rate of inflation, or the rate of change in prices is measured by the use of a **price index.** Over a period of time some prices may rise considerably, others hardly at all and the prices of some goods may fall. An index of prices attempts to gauge the effect of all price changes by attaching most importance to the prices of those goods on which people spend most money. This is done by 'weighting' each item or group of items; the weight is dependent on the volume of spending on each item. A simple example can illustrate the advantage of such a method. Suppose there exist two goods, and only two goods which people buy, meat and bread; if the price of meat rose by 50 % and the price of bread by 10 %, then it could be stated that the average price rise was 30 %. However, this takes no account of the relative importance of the two goods in consumers' spending patterns, for if people spend 80 % of their income on meat and only 20 % on bread, then the rise in the prices paid by consumers is in excess of 30 %. The weighted price rise is calculated by first weighting each product, and in this case, if the total weighting is to be 100, then meat must have a weight of 80 and bread must have a weight of 20. The original price of each item is then given an index of 100 at the starting date (also called the base date). Thus a rise in price of 50 % will raise the index to 150, a 20 % fall in price would reduce the index to 80. The weighted price change can be measured using the same method as is used in the following table.

Item	Price increase	Index number	Weight	Index × Weight
Meat	50 %	150	80	12000
Bread	10 %	110	20	2200
				14200

$$\textbf{Weighted price level} = \frac{14200}{100} = \textbf{142}$$

The new weighted price level is 142, this means that prices have risen, not by 30 % as was calculated previously, but by 42 %.

The Retail Price index

Changes in prices paid by the general public are measured by the retail price index (RPI). The RPI is the overall change in the cost of a basket of goods and is expressed in index form by taking the cost of the basket at the starting date (the base date) of January 1974, as equal to 100.

The index measures the month by month change in the prices of the large majority of goods and services that households buy. Thus the index excludes income tax and national insurance payments but does include the effect of expenditure taxes and subsidies, since these are included in retail prices.

	1974	1977	1981
All items	1,000	1,000	1,000
Food	232	247	207
Alcoholic drink	82	83	79
Tobacco	46	46	36
Housing	108	112	135
Fuel and light	53	58	62
Durable household goods	70	63	65
Clothing and footwear	89	82	81
Transport and vehicles	149	139	152
Miscellaneous goods	71	71	75
Services	52	54	66
Meals outside home	48	45	42

Table 28. The changing composition of the RPI (1974 to 1981).

The composition of the basket is based on information from the Family Expenditure Survey which is a detailed continuous survey of the spending patterns of 7,000 households each year, at a rate of 270 every fortnight. Each January the composition of the basket is brought up to date to allow for changes in the overall spending pattern of the community. The basket is given a total weighting of 1,000, Table 28, shows how the weighting of various items has changed over the last few years.

Once the composition of the basket is formulated, changes in the cost of the basket can be calculated. Some 150,000 price quotations are obtained each month from retailers throughout the country, and from these quotations changes in the prices of each item or group of items are estimated.

Table 29 illustrates the general rise in the RPI during 1981 of 11·9%, but also shows how the price rises of the individual items ranged from tobacco (23·5%) to clothing and footwear (1·4%).

Item	Weight	Percentage increase in retail prices
Food	207	8·4
Alcoholic drink	79	16·9
Tobacco	36	23·9
Housing	135	18·1
Fuel and light	62	21·3
Durable household goods	65	4·8
Clothing and footwear	81	1·4
Transport and vehicles	152	11·7
Miscellaneous goods	75	8·8
Services	66	14·5
Meals outside home	42	9·6
All items	1,000	11·9

Table 29. Retail prices index (effective weight 1,000*) price rises January to December 1981.*

A special price index is prepared for both single pensioners and pensioner couples, and this determines the increase in the pension. There is also an index which reflects the prices paid by firms, the Wholesale Prices Index (WPI).

Types of inflation

Economists have tended to distinguish between two types of inflation (a) creeping inflation and (b) hyperinflation.

(a) Creeping or moderate inflation is a process of gently rising prices of about 2% to 4% per year. This is the level of inflation experienced by the world's industrial nations between 1945 and 1970. It is claimed that creeping inflation has the advantage of encouraging investment, as investors can expect rising profits. The logic behind this is disputable.

(b) Hyperinflation is a process in which prices are completely out of control, and where prices may double or quadruple every day. Germany suffered from this type of inflation during 1923, and at times prices were doubling every hour. In 1944 Hungary suffered an even more severe inflation.

The effects of inflation

1. Redistribution of income

Inflation redistributes income between members of the community. Some parts of the community are able to obtain the higher incomes necessary to pay the higher prices, whereas those on fixed incomes, and those who are unable to obtain higher money incomes suffer a reduction in their real income, and their standard of living. Firms are usually able to increase their profits during periods of inflation, and workers in strong trade unions may be able to obtain the wage increases needed to compensate for inflation. Until 1974, pensioners suffered from inflation because they were unable to obtain higher pensions to pay the higher prices, but the Labour government introduced a system whereby pensions are protected against inflation.

2. Employment and production

If the United Kingdom has a rate of inflation which is higher than that of her international trading partners, then the prices of British goods will rise faster than the prices of foreign goods. This will have several consequences.

The demand for British goods will fall both at home and abroad. Firms will cut back on production and this may necessitate redundancies and lay-offs, thus increasing the level of unemployment.

3. The balance of payments

More foreign goods will be sold in the U.K. as their prices will be lower than the prices of British goods, and as Britain will be selling fewer goods abroad this will lead to a deficit in the balance of payments. This will initially be financed by a reduction in Britain's holdings of gold and foreign currencies, but if the situation continues the value of sterling will fall.

The causes of inflation

There are considered to be two main causes of inflation: (a) Monetary demand pull and (b) cost push.

(a) Monetary demand pull

If at the ruling market price the monetary demand for a product exceeds the supply, the price of the good will rise. Monetary demand pull inflation is a situation where the level of monetary demand for all goods and services exceeds supply with the result that the prices of all goods rise. The rate of change of the money supply is seen as being the major determinant of the rate of inflation. Changes in the money supply are considerably affected by government monetary and fiscal policies. Vote seeking governments are frequently tempted to increase their spending without increasing taxation—the deficit is then financed by printing bank notes and borrowing. However, both of these methods will cause an increase in the money supply either directly or indirectly through the banking system. During the mid 1970s both Conservative and Labour governments allowed large increases in their spending without increasing taxation thus increasing the level of monetary demand in the economy and inflation. This theory of inflation suggests that a tight control of the money supply would be an appropriate anti-inflation policy.

(b) Cost push inflation

Firms may increase their prices in response to increases in costs. The major elements of costs are labour and raw materials, and as Britain imports a large proportion of the raw materials used in production, cost inflation has been described both as wage inflation and imported inflation.

Wage inflation occurs when workers obtain wage increases higher than increases in productivity. Trade unions have been accused of causing wage inflation by making excessive wage demands and by using the strike weapon too readily to support their claims.

Imported inflation not only raises the prices of raw materials, but raises the prices of imported consumer goods. Large increases in the prices of imports occurred in the mid 1970s. In 1974 the price of imported goods rose by 55·5%, and the price of imported oil quadrupled.

The two main causes of inflation work hand in hand with each other. For example, if trade unions succeed in obtaining high wage increases then this will stimulate cost inflation as firms will try to protect their profits by raising prices. At the same time workers will wish to spend their increased money, but if the supply of goods is the same as before, then the average price of goods and services will be raised by the excess demand.

Anti-inflation policies

There are two basic types of policy to attack inflation, and the choice of policy is determined by the cause thought to be responsible. If monetary demand pull is thought to be the cause then a strict control of the monetary conditions in the country is advocated. This primarily involves some control of the money supply through a tight control of government borrowing, bank lending and usually hire purchase controls.

Wage inflation is attacked through prices and incomes policies, which are designed to control increases in incomes and prices. Britain has used various incomes policies in an attempt to control inflation.

Imported inflation is the most difficult to control. It is worsened by a deteriorating exchange rate, but an improving exchange rate reduces the effects of increases in the price of imports.

Key terms

Inflation is an increase in the general level of prices. The rate of inflation is measured by a price index.

The Retail Price Index measures changes in the prices paid by the general public.

Creeping inflation is a process of gently rising prices.

Hyperinflation is where prices are completely out of control.

Monetary demand pull inflation is caused by the level of monetary demand in the economy exceeding the supply of goods and services.

Wage inflation is caused by wage increases in excess of increases in productivity which forces firms to raise prices.

Imported inflation is caused by increases in the prices of imported goods.

Chapter 14
Banking and Finance

The money market

The money market, which is also called the discount market, is a market for short-term loans, usually of less than three months duration, required by companies and the government.

Treasury bills

To finance its spending the government requires short-term loans. Each Friday the government offers a certain quantity of Treasury bills for sale to the public and to the discount houses in units of £5,000 and £10,000 for 91 days. That is, the government will repay the holder the money value of the bill in 91 days. Those tendering for these bills will offer a certain amont of cash now for the specified amount in the future. This process is called discounting. For example a tender of £9,600 for a £10,000 Treasury bill for 91 days represents a discount rate (a rate of interest) of about 16% per annum. The lower the amount offered by the tender, the higher the rate of interest that the lender is receiving and the higher the rate of interest the government is paying. The Treasury offers the bills to the highest bidder, and thus pays the lowest rate of interest.

Commercial bills

Commercial bills (also called **bills of exchange**) are discounted by the discount houses in the same way as they discount Treasury bills, the main difference being that commercial bills are used by companies. At one time bills of exchange provided a large part of the business of the discount houses, as they were used by importers and exporters to finance international trade. However, the increased use of the cheque, and other methods of international payments has reduced the use of these bills substantially.

Discount houses

The Discount houses (of which there are 11) initially provide the short-term finance by discounting Treasury bills and bills of exchange. They in turn obtain their funds from the commercial banks. Commercial banks are prepared to lend to the discount houses at a low rate of interest if they can be repaid at very short notice. This type of loan enables the commercial banks to obtain interest on any excesses of cash whilst being able to recall the money at short notice if necessary. Sometimes the discount houses cannot obtain the funds they need from the banks, or the banks may recall their loans. In this case the discount houses can borrow from the Bank of England, but usually at a higher rate of interest. This function of the Bank of England has led to it being called '*the lender of last resort*'.

The discount houses make a profit by the difference in interest rates that they charge for lending and that they pay to the commercial banks for the finance that they obtain.

The Commercial Banks

The large majority of commercial banking business is carried out in the United Kingdom by members of the Committee of London Clearing banks. These consist of the 'Big Four' – Barclays, Lloyds, Midland and National Westminster. Other members of the Clearing House are Williams and Glyn's, Coutts and Co., the Cooperative Bank and the Trustees Savings Bank.

The commercial banks provide banking services throughout Britain, and operate about 14,000 branches; 11,000 of these are run by the 'Big Four'.

The main functions of the commercial banks are as follows:

1. Accepting deposits

Banks accept deposits from their customers into current accounts and deposit accounts. Deposits into current accounts can be withdrawn on demand and do not usually earn interest. Banks usually make a charge for current accounts unless a minimum amount is kept in the account (between £50 and £100). Current account deposits can be transferred by cheque.

Deposit accounts cannot always be withdrawn on demand, (a depositor may have to wait a few days for large amounts) and they cannot be transferred by cheque. Interest is paid on these accounts.

2. Lending

Banks provide loans for private individuals and firms. Traditionally banks have only supplied short-term finance for firms, but in recent years the banks have expanded the scope of their activities and are now prepared to make medium term loans. Banks make their profits by the difference in the interest rates they pay to their depositors and charge their borrowers.

3. Transferring deposits

The large majority of payments are made by cheque, and the commercial banks handle millions of cheques every year. If a payment is made by cheque from Smith to Jones for £10, the bank reduces Smith's current account by £10, and increases the deposit in Jones' current account by £10 – no money changes hands. With a banking system that contains several banks the process becomes slightly more complex as banks have to transfer money. Each bank totals the claims of its own depositors on the other banks, and only the difference between the claims of each need to be transferred. Thus if Bank A has claims of £6 million on deposits of Bank B, and Bank B's depositors have claims of £5 million on deposits in Bank A, then only £1 million needs to be transferred from Bank A to Bank B.

This process is performed in Britain through the **Bankers' Clearing House** whereby the six clearing banks exchange cheques and pay or receive the differences. As the commercial banks themselves have accounts at the Bank of England, these payments are made by transferring the amounts between these deposits.

4. Other services

The banks provide a wide range of other services for their customers including specialist advice on such matters as taxation and investment, the provision of credit cards and cheque cards, and obtaining foreign exchange.

5. The creation of credit

Only a small fraction of the deposits held by banks are required in the form of cash. This fact means that banks are able to create money. Suppose the deposits in a bank total £100, and that the bank knows that only £10 will be required in the form of cash at any one time. The bank can therefore lend out a further £900 (by putting £900 in the accounts of borrowers) thus having total deposits of £1,000. The £100 that it has in cash will be sufficient to satisfy the demands for cash. This creation of credit is highly profitable for the banks, as they can charge interest on the £900 of deposits that it has created. Any increase in deposits can mean that bank lending can increase by a further nine times.

To ensure that the banks do not create too great an amount – with the result that it would have insufficient cash to cover its needs there is a very strict control of bank lending by the Bank of England. A new system of monetary control was introduced in 1981. Since 1971 the banks had had to keep $12\frac{1}{2}$% of their assets in liquid form – this was called the reserve assets ratio. In January 1981 the Bank of England reduced the reserve assets ratio to 10% after it had announced that this would be phased out as it was not necessary for monetary control (see Monetary Control, below).

The Bank of England

The Bank of England was founded in 1694 to manage the government's debt. It became accepted as the nation's central bank during the nineteenth century and now stands at the centre of the British banking system. The Bank was nationalized in 1946 by the Bank of England Act.

The functions of the Bank of England

1. The note issue

The Issue Department of the Bank controls the issuing of notes. The Bank prints and releases notes into the economy in relation to its needs. The Bank of England is the sole issuing authority in England and Wales.

2. Banker to the government

The Bank of England services the accounts of the Exchequer and the central government departments in the same way that a commercial bank services a private account. It receives revenue and pays out expenditure. It also advises the government in financial policy.

The two most important functions as government's banker are the managing of the national debt, and conducting international transactions through the *Exchange Equalization Account* (EEA), and by acting as the government's agent to international financial institutions, such as the International Monetary Fund (IMF). The Bank manages the national debt by issuing securities on behalf of the government, repaying any maturing securities and paying interest to bond holders. Revenue is received from taxation at irregular intervals by the government and short term loans in the form of Treasury bills are issued weekly to ensure that a regular flow of funds is available to meet government expenditures. The Bank manages the EEA on behalf of the Treasury. This account holds the nation's reserves of gold and foreign currencies and is used to maintain the value of the pound in the foreign exchange market.

3. Banker to the commercial banks

The commercial banks, overseas banks, finance houses and discount houses maintain accounts at the Bank, and this enables them to transfer money between each other. By controlling the deposits of the commercial banks the Bank of England is able to influence the level of bank lending.

4. Monetary policy

The bank manages the country's monetary system on behalf of the government so as to implement the government's monetary policy. This function is examined in greater detail under the heading monetary control.

Other controls

Other controls on the availability of credit can be made by the government. The Treasury can enforce hire purchase controls to place maximum repayment periods and minimum deposits on instalment credit. As instalment credit is an important factor in the purchase of consumer durables, such action will reduce the level of demand in the economy.

The capital market

The capital market provides the capital that is needed by firms and government to finance circulating capital and fixed capital. Short-term capital is normally provided by the banks which make loans, and allow firms to run overdrafts; and also through the discount market and through trade creditors – these are suppliers of goods and materials who are prepared to wait for payment. Long-term capital is obtained from the capital market. The sources of long-term finance for firms are examined in detail in Chapter 5 (pages 44 to 46), and are listed below.

1. Retained profits.
2. Shares.
3. Debentures.
4. Specialist sources of finance – Finance for Industry, Equity Capital for Industry and the British Technology Group.

The nationalized industries obtain finance for capital investment from internal sources and interest-bearing loans from the Exchequer.

Monetary control

Monetary policy is used by the government to influence the level of economic activity and the Bank implements this policy. The role of the Bank is important since it can influence the ability of the commercial banks and the other financial institutions to lend. The present government has emphasised the importance of control of the money supply as a tool of policy. The Bank seeks to influence the trend of the growth of the money supply in accordance with target rates of growth. These targets are incorporated in the medium term financial strategy. The methods by which the Bank operates in the money markets have undergone some change and nowadays the Bank influences monetary conditions mainly through its dealings with the discount houses and open market operations.

If the Bank wishes to withdraw cash from the banking system it sells government securities in the open market. The buyers pay for the securities with cheques drawn on the commercial banks; bank deposits fall in the process and the banks will have to reduce their lending. If the banking system is short of funds the Bank relieves the shortage either by buying bills from the discount houses or by lending directly to them.

Until August 1981 the Bank lent directly to the discount houses at rates at or near its announced Minimum Lending Rate, in addition to its open-market dealings with the discount houses in bills.

Under the new arrangements, the Bank no longer undertakes to announce continuously the rate at which it will supply cash to the Market, but conducts its operations in such a way as to keep short-term interest rates within a published band. More emphasis is now being put on open-market operation in bills than on direct lending to the discount houses.

The Stock Exchange

The twenty-four stock exchanges of the United Kingdom and Irish Republic amalgamated in 1973 to become The Stock Exchange with its centre in London. The Stock exchange is the market for the buying and selling of second-hand securities, and at the end of March 1981 about 7,300 securities were quoted on the Stock Exchange and they had a total market value of £376,000 million. The Stock Exchange does not trade in securities, nor does it fix their prices; it provides a central efficient market where members of the Stock Exchange can trade. Three types of security are traded on the Stock Exchange.

1. **Gilt-edged securities,** which are bonds issued by the U.K. government.
2. **Debentures** which are loan stocks issued by companies, and other loan stock issued by foreign governments and local authorities.
3. **Shares of public companies.** Both ordinary and preference shares are traded (see Chapter 5).

More than four fifths of the securities are issued by companies. There are about 4,000 members of the Stock Exchange, and only members are allowed on the trading floor of the Exchange. About a third of all members are jobbers, and the remainder are brokers.

Brokers act on behalf of members of the public, and charge a fee for their services. **Jobbers** do not trade with members of the public, and can be compared to wholesalers, but who trade in securities. Jobbers act on their own behalf by trading with brokers, making a profit by the difference between their buying and selling prices. Jobbers specialize in particular groups of shares such as chemicals, oil, engineering or gilt-edged.

When a member of the public wishes to buy or sell securities he approaches a broker and instructs him to buy or sell within a given price range. The broker will approach a jobber who specializes in that type of security, and will ask the price of that security. The jobber will give him two prices – the price at which he will buy the security and the price at which he will sell. If the price is satisfactory the deal will be made.

Speculation

Speculators attempt to gain a profit by anticipating the price movements of shares, and buying and selling accordingly. A bull is a speculator who hopes that the price of the security will rise so that he can sell at a profit. A bear is a speculator who agrees to supply a security at a particular price, and hopes that the price will fall before he has to purchase and deliver the security.

The main value of the Stock Exchange is that it facilitates borrowing by the government and companies. Although new issues are not traded an investor will be more prepared to purchase a new issue if he knows that he will be able to sell them again at any time.

Ways of saving

The savings of individuals, firms and institutions can be directed to manufacturing and commercial enterprises, where they provide circulating and fixed capital, and earn a rate of interest for the investors.

Some of the main methods of saving are listed below:

1. **Banks** offer current accounts which are mainly used for transactionary purposes and deposit accounts which yield interest.

2. **Building Societies** offer a wide range of saving methods. The object of saving with a Building Society is often with a view to using the money saved as a deposit on a house being purchased, the balance being provided by a mortgage from the society. However, building societies compete with other institutions by offering fixed term deposits for which the annual rate of interest rises with longer periods of investment.

3. **National Savings.** A variety of government savings schemes are administered by the Department of National Savings:

National Savings Bank accounts, National Savings Certificates, British Savings Bonds, Premium Savings Bonds and Save as you Earn contracts. In May 1981 the total investment in all forms of National Savings Certificate was £9,500 million; and sales of premium bonds to May 1981 were £1,470 million.

4. The Trustees Savings Bank comprises 16 individual banks with about 1,650 branches and in June 1981 had 14 million accounts and total deposits in excess of £5,700 million.

5. Shares of public companies yield interest depending on profit levels; these shares are bought through the Stock Exchange.

6. Government securities (gilt-edged stock) yield a yearly fixed return, but the rate of interest on bonds tends to be low.

7. Finance Houses, which engage in financing instalment credit accept deposits from the public and pay interest on such deposits.

8. Unit Trusts and Investment Trusts invest savings over a range of stocks and shares and enable investors to spread their risks, and also obtain the benefit of skilled management.

9. Insurance companies and Mutual Societies operate savings schemes, usually tied to a life assurance policy. Endowment policies allow savers to invest over a specified number of years, and the policy will be paid on the death of the insurer or on the date of maturity.

10. Local Authority bonds provide an annual rate of interest for investors; the finance raised is used for capital projects such as the building of schools and fire stations.

Key terms

The money market is the market for short-term loans, usually of less than three months duration required by the government and companies.

The capital market is the market for long-term loans required by firms to finance spending on fixed capital.

Discount houses provide short-term loans to the money market.

Commercial banks carry out the large majority of commercial banking business, carrying out a wide range of functions.

The Bank of England is the nation's central bank and stands at the centre of the British banking system.

Monetary policy refers to government action to influence the level of economic activity by influencing the cost and availability of credit.

Monetary control is achieved primarily through the use of open market operation and by direct lending to the discount houses.

The Stock Exchange is the market for second-hand securities.

Chapter 15
National Income

A. Measurement of the national income

National income is the total output of goods and services produced in an economy over a period of time, normally one year, and represented in money values. There are three ways of calculating the national income:

1. **The Income method**
2. **The Expenditure method**
3. **The Output method**

The result given by each of these methods should be the same, as the total incomes of the community earned in producing the output should be equal to the value of the output of goods and services, which in turn must equal the total expenditures on the goods and services produced.

National Income = National Expenditure = National Output

Precise measurements of the National Income of the United Kingdom are made by the Central Statistical Office and these are published annually in '*National Income and Expenditure*' commonly referred to as the Blue Book.

1. The Income method

The calculation of the national income using the income method is shown in Table 30. Basically, this is the addition of incomes received as result of domestic production. However, not all incomes are included for some incomes are received which do not represent the production of goods or services. The pensioner's income, for example, does not represent a certain quantity of work performed, neither does the widow's pension or the child benefit allowance. These are all **transfer payments** and they are not included in the calculation of the national income. The guide to whether an income should be included is to ask whether the income is a return for a service provided in the productive process.

Stock appreciation. As the profits of companies and corporations are included (since they would have formed part of income had the firms distributed them to their shareholders or workers), it is necessary to deduct stock appreciation. Stock appreciation is the increase in the money values of stocks held by firms, which is deducted since it does not represent a real increase in the income of the community.

1980	£ million
Income from employment	137,083
Gross trading profits of companies	23,644
Gross trading surplus of public corporations	6,015
Gross trading surplus of general government enterprises	170
Other income	33,763
Stock appreciation	–6,477
Residual error	–1,062
Gross Domestic Product (GDP)	193,136
Net property income from abroad	–112
Gross National Product (GNP)	193,024
less Capital consumption	
National income	

Table 30. The calculation of the national income using the income method (1980)

Net property income from abroad. Some of the income received by British residents does not only arise from domestic production but from abroad, if they have investments outside the U.K. This item measures the net effect of income entering and leaving the country in the form of interest payments, rents and dividends.

GNP = GDP + net property income from abroad

Capital consumption. During the production of goods and services fixed capital is used up. By subtracting Capital consumption the net output of the nation is obtained.

National income = GNP – Capital consumption

2. The Expenditure method

The calculation of the national income using the expenditure method is shown in Table 31. Basically, this is the sum of all expenditures. However certain important points must be noted.

1980	£ million
Consumers' expenditure	135,403
General government final consumption	48,285
Gross domestic fixed capital formation	40,050
Value of physical increase in stocks and work in progress	−3,886
Total domestic expenditure	219,852
Exports of goods and services	63,188
Imports of goods and services	−57,832
GDP (market prices)	255,208
Taxes less subsidies	−32,072
GDP (factor cost)	193,136
Net property income from abroad	−112
GNP (factor cost)	193,024
less Capital consumption	
National income	

Table 31. The calculation of the national income using the Expenditure method (1980)

Factor cost and market prices. The available statistics on expenditure do not show the cost of goods and services, rather they show the prices of goods after indirect taxes have been added, and subsidies have been paid. This means that indirect taxes net of subsidies will have to be subtracted if national income is to be calculated.

Imports and Exports. If we are trying to calculate the output of goods and services in the U.K. economy then we must take account of the fact that many of the goods bought in Britain are imported and that some of the U.K.'s production of goods and services is sold abroad. It is necessary therefore to add exports and subtract imports.

Government consumption. The government not only spends money on goods and services (i.e. hospitals, schools) it also spends on transfer payments. As transfer payments are not included in the calculation of the national income, they are subtracted from government expenditure before the table is compiled.

Industry	1980 £ million	Per cent
Agriculture, forestry, fishing	4,296	2·2
Petroleum and natural gas	7,649	4·0
Other mining and quarrying	3,222	1·7
Manufacturing	48,060	24·8
Construction	13,025	6·7
Gas, electricity and water	5,803	3·0
Transport	10,084	5·2
Communication	5,326	2·8
Distributive trades	19,328	10·0
Insurance, banking and finance	18,288	9·5
Ownership of dwellings	11,996	6·2
Professional and Scientific Services	25,467	13·2
Miscellaneous services	18,734	9·7
Public administration and defence	13,987	7·2
Adjustment for financial services	−9,732	−5·0
Residual error	−2,045	−1·1
Gross domestic product at factor cost	193,488	100·0

Table 32. Calculation of Gross domestic product by industry (1980)

3. The Output method

The calculation of the national income using the output method is shown in Table 32. The output of all industries is added to give the GDP at factor cost. Two important points must be noted.

Double counting. If the output of all industries were simply added together we would have a result greater than the actual output of the economy, since we would count the output of some goods and services more than once. For example, suppose a manufacturer of car components sells starter motors to a car assembly plant. If the output of the car component firm and the car assembly firm are both added then the starter motor will have been added twice. To avoid double counting the value-added approach is used. To obtain the value added output of an industry, inputs from other industries are deducted from gross output.

Adjustment for financial services. It is impossible to allocate certain financial services in calculating value added output, so that although the total output of financial services is known the exact allocation between the other industries cannot be calculated. Adjustment for financial services is illustrated in Table 32.

By using the calculation of GDP as calculated above, it is now possible to calculate national income, as in Tables 30 and 31.

B. The use of national income statistics

1. Changes in national income. The national income statistics can be used to measure changes in national income. To do this the effects of inflation must be removed. An economy might have a national income of £100 in Year 1 and £110 in Year 2; however, if the nation has experienced a rate of inflation of 10%, then the **real national income** is unchanged, it is only the effects of inflation which have raised **money national income.** So in comparing national income over time the effects of inflation must be removed. A second problem arising in the comparison of national income over time is that of **population.** If real national income rose from £100 in Year 1 to £110 in Year 2 then real national income has risen by 10%, but if the population has risen by 10%, then the real national income per head is unchanged. Output per head is important when examining the standard of living.
2. International comparisons. The national income statistics can be used to make comparisons between nations, but some problems arise because the basis on which the statistics are calculated may be different. Some countries have great difficulties in obtaining the statistics because there is a high degree of illiteracy in the population. International comparisons use the output per head as a guide to comparative living standards, but this does not necessarily reflect the standard of living of the people because of differences in the **distribution of income.** In some of the *oil states* of the Middle East the income per head is high but the standard of living of the mass of the population is low. International comparisons are made on the basis of the **exchange rates** in different countries, but this is also subject to error since this approach assumes that relative price levels are the same. **Climatic differences** can also affect relative living standards. A cold country may require a higher income per head than warm countries to achieve the same standard of living since the population of the warm country will not have to budget so heavily for heating.

C. The determination of national income

It is possible to construct a simplified model of the economy to help us to understand the way in which the economy works, and how the level of national income is determined. Such a model is shown in Figure 27. The model shows the circular flow of income between the two main sectors within the economy – the Produc-

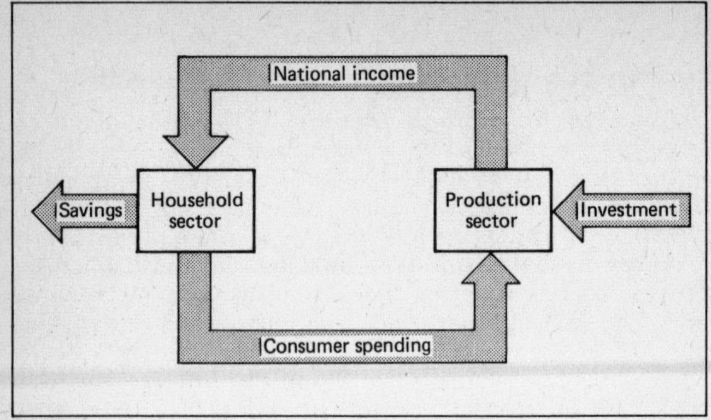

Figure 27. The Circular Flow of income.

tion sector and the Household sector. For simplicity we assume a closed economy with no government sector. The Production sector produces consumer goods and services, in response to demand from consumers (C) and investment goods from firms (I). Investment is an injection into the circular flow since this is income which does not originate with the model.

The Production sector uses all its sales receipts to purchase factors of production from the household sector – labour and land for example.

The Household sector receives payments from the Production sector for the factor services provided in the form of wages, rent, interest and profits. The Household can either spend this income on the goods and services produced by the Production sector or it can save it. Saving is clearly a leakage from the circular flow.

Equilibrium National Income

Equilibrium national income is that level of income where there is no tendency for income to change. By referring to Figure 27 it can be seen that national income will be in equilibrium when (a) injections equal leakages ($I = S$) (b) the output of goods is equal to the demand for that output ($Y = C + I$).

The Determination of Equilibrium National Income

A hypothetical example can illustrate the determination of equilibrium national income in a simple economy.

National Income (£) (Y)	Consumer Spending (£) (C)	Saving (£) (S)	Investment (£) (I)
100	90	10	30
200	180	20	30
300	270	30	30
400	360	40	30
500	450	50	30

Let us suppose that national income is currently £100, the community spends £90 on consumer goods and services and saves £10. The business sector is currently investing in new capital at a rate of £30. The economy is not in equilibrium since

(a) Investment exceeds Savings ($I > S$),

(b) The demand for current output exceeds current output ($Y < C+I$).

Simply, the economy is producing goods and services worth £100, but the demand for output is £120 (£90 consumer goods and £30 investment goods). Firms will find their stocks of unsold goods falling and will respond by increasing output; to increase output they will need to buy more factor services from the household sector and therefore income will rise. Income and output will continue to rise until Savings and Investment are equal where national income is £300.

Alternatively, if national income is currently £500 then firms' current output exceeds the demand for that output; stocks of unsold goods will rise and firms will react by cutting back output and income. Equilibrium will once again be reached when Investment = Savings ($I = S$) and the demand for current output equals current output ($Y = C+I$); where Y = £300.

Changes in Equilibrium National Income

A change in equilibrium national income can be brought about by a change in one or more of the variables C, S or I.

A rise in investment would increase demand and would therefore lead to a rise in national income. A fall in investment would reduce national income.

A rise in saving will increase leakages and will cause a fall in demand – this will lead to a fall in output and a fall in equilibrium national income. A fall in saving will reduce leakages and therefore cause an increase in consumer demand – this will lead to a rise in output and a rise in equilibrium national income.

Chapter 16
The Public Sector

In 1977, the state in the form of central government, local government and the nationalised industries, employed 28·5% of the U.K. workforce. Total Government Expenditure was £61,964 millions, which represented almost 45% of Gross National Product. This expenditure was mainly financed from taxation – which totalled £51,095 millions, the remainder coming from various sources, in particular government borrowing. The simplest way to examine the public sector is by discussing government expenditure and government revenue separately, beginning with expenditure.

Government Expenditure

The reasons for government expenditure can be grouped into four basic categories:

1. The provision of public goods. There are certain services, called 'public goods' which the government has to provide because private firms will be unwilling or unable to do so. Suppose that a firm decides to build a lighthouse on some very dangerous rocks to reduce the number of ships being sunk. An individual ship-owner could receive the benefit of the lighthouse (as his ship would be less likely to hit the rocks), without paying for this service, because the lighthouse owners would have no way of making him pay. Therefore, private firms will refuse to operate lighthouses because they will be unable to make a profit. If the community wishes to have lighthouses in operation, then the government will have to intervene by operating the lighthouses and raising the money to pay for them by taxation.

Public goods such as lighthouses are quite rare, other examples are National Defence, i.e. the Armed Services, the Police Force and the Judiciary. At one time, spending on public goods made up almost all government expenditure, but in recent years this has fallen as a percentage and nowadays accounts for only about 20% of total government spending.

2. The provision of social services. The largest aspect of government spending is expenditure on social services, and in particular on health, education and housing. The reasoning behind such expenditure is the belief that everyone is entitled to certain facilities regardless of their income or status. If the provision of these were left entirely to private firms, it is generally believed that people with low incomes would have to do without them, and thus some people would be homeless, uneducated, and would not receive medical treatment if they fell ill. Other social service spending includes retirement pensions, maternity benefits, child benefit, widow's allowance, sickness benefit, unemployment benefit and supplementary benefits.

3. To increase industrial efficiency. The government attempts to influence the industrial efficiency of the economy in two main ways. Firstly, the belief that certain industries are more efficient under public ownership has led to the nationalization of certain sectors (see Chapter 4). Secondly, the state can use public funds to attempt to improve the performance of the private sector. The Industry Acts of 1972 and 1975 encourage capital expenditure on plant and machinery by providing grants and tax allowances. Other financial incentives are available for firms where it is considered to be in the national interest.

4. To influence the level of economic activity. Public expenditure, in conjunction with taxation and monetary policy, has an important influence on the level of economic activity in the country. An increase in the level of public spending can reduce unemployment. On the other hand, a reduction in public expenditure can reduce the level of demand in the economy, increase unemployment and reduce inflation.

The Structure of Public Expenditure

Since 1945 government spending has increased as the state has widened the scope of its activities. There has been a general decline in expenditure on defence as a percentage of public expenditure and this reflects Britain's reduced commitments overseas. The major increases in public spending have been in the social services. An increasing school population until 1980, and the expansion of the numbers who remain in full time education after the school leaving age have required increased spending on education. The increasing numbers of pensioners and a rising level of unemployment have raised the level of spending on social security benefits considerably. The structure of public spending has thus been moving towards the social services. The present Conservative government has attempted to redress the balance towards defence and law and order, but increased spending on social security due to higher unemployment has made their task difficult.

Expenditure	1981–82 £000m	Per cent
Social Security	28·2	23·6
Health and personal social services	15·5	13·0
Education, Science, arts and libraries	14·1	11·8
Defence	12·3	10·3
Housing	5·5	4·6
Other environmental services	4·9	4·1
Law, order and protective services	4·4	3·7
Transport	3·7	3·1
Industry, energy, trade	3·1	2·6
Employment	2·4	2·0
Nationalised industries' borrowing	2·4	2·0
Overseas aid and services	2·0	1·7
Agriculture, fisheries, food and forestry	1·5	1·2
Other public services	3·0	2·5
Contingency reserve	1·6	1·3
Special sales of assets	−0·2	−0·2
General government debt interest	13·3	11·0
Other	2·0	1·7
General government expenditure	119·5	100·0

Table 33. General government expenditure (1981–82)

Public Revenue

In the financial year 1981–82 General government receipts and borrowing amounted to £119·5 billion, raised as follows:

Source of revenue	£ billion	Per cent
Central government taxation	74·0	61·8
National Insurance, etc, contributions	17·0	14·2
Local authority rates	10·9	9·1
Trading income, rent, interest	7·4	6·2
General government borrowing	10·4	8·7
General government receipts	119·5	100·0

Table 34. General government receipts and borrowing (1981–82)

Taxation

The major source of public revenue is taxation. The principal objectives of taxation in the United Kingdom today are:

1. To raise revenue. The traditional purpose of taxation was to raise revenue to finance spending on 'public goods', particularly defence. The growth of public spending in other areas has meant that this objective remains the major objective of taxation, although nowadays other functions are also important.

2. The management of the economy. Since the end of the Second World War, governments have attempted to maintain economic stability, and taxation is an important instrument in carrying out this task. Governments can, for example, attempt to reduce the level of unemployment by reducing taxation, and thus raising the level of demand in the economy.

3. The redistribution of income and wealth. Redistribution usually refers to the transfer of income and wealth from the richer sections of the community to the poorer sections of the community. Important distinctions can be made concerning the effect of a tax on the distribution of income.

A tax is said to be *proportional* if the tax is levied in direct proportion to income, i.e. a proportional tax would take £1 from a person earning £10 and £100 from a person earning £1,000.

A tax is called *progressive* if it takes an increasing proportion of income, as income rises. A tax which takes £1 from a person earning £100, and £100 from a person earning £1,000 is progressive because the lower income is taxed at 1%, and the higher income at 10%. Income tax is the most important of the progressive taxes in operation in the United Kingdom.

A tax is termed *regressive* if it takes a decreasing proportion of income, as income rises. A tax which takes £10 from a person earning £100, and £10 from a person earning £1,000 is a regressive tax since the tax rate declines as income rises, from 10% for the lower income earner to 1% for the higher income earner. Value Added Tax (VAT) is a regressive tax.

If the object of a tax system is to redistribute income from the rich to the poor, then a system of progressive taxes should prevail.

4. To influence specific expenditures. Governments often wish to influence spending on specific items, and may use a tax for this purpose. Governments have attempted to reduce the demand for petrol and cigarettes by increasing the tax on these items. The government can encourage spending on a particular good by taxing its substitutes. Thus, heating oils were taxed to increase the demand for coal.

The principles of taxation

In 1776 Adam Smith laid down four principles of taxation, which he termed 'the canons of taxation'. He considered that a tax should follow certain basic principles.

(1) Equity. Taxes should be levied so that the burden of taxation should be apportioned according to the ability to pay. Today it is believed that the most equitable taxes are progressive taxes.

(2) Certainty. The contributor should be certain of the method, amount and time of payment. That is, taxes should be simple to understand and difficult to evade.

(3) Economy. A tax should be economic to operate and should be neither a disincentive to effort nor harmful to the production of a product, unless that is the particular objective of the tax.

(4) Convenience. Taxes should be levied and collected in a way that is convenient for the taxpayer.

Although other principles have been added to this list, these remain the most important principles of taxation.

The classification of taxes

Taxes are often classified as either *direct* or *indirect*.

A direct tax is a tax which is levied directly on income, wealth or property.

An indirect tax is a tax levied on goods and services, and which the contributor pays indirectly to the taxing authority, in the form of a higher price for the good or service.

In the United Kingdom taxes on income and wealth are considered to be direct taxes, and these taxes are collected by the Inland Revenue.

Taxes on expenditure are usually considered to be indirect taxes in the United Kingdom, and these consist of a host of central government taxes, such as VAT and tobacco tax. Most of these are collected by H.M. Customs and Excise. Local taxes in the form of the 'rates' are collected by local authorities.

The structure of taxation

There are three main types of taxation:

(a) Taxes on income.
(b) Taxes on capital and wealth.
(c) Taxes on spending.

If the contributions of employers and employees in National Insurance and Health payments are considered the composition of the tax burden in 1981–82 was as in Table 35.

(a) Taxes on income

The main taxes on income are Income tax, which is levied on private individuals and unincorporated businesses, and Corporation tax which is levied on companies.

Tax	£ billion	Per cent
Central government taxation	74·0	72·6
National insurance, etc, contributions	10·9	10·7
Local authority rates	17·0	16·6
Total	101·9	100·0

Table 35. Composition of the tax burden (1981–82)

Income tax

Income tax was first introduced during the Napoleonic Wars, but was later withdrawn, it was reimposed in 1842 at a rate of 3%. Broadly speaking, income tax is charged on all income accruing to individuals resident in the United Kingdom. Every individual has a tax-free allowance, that is, a certain level of income which is not subject to tax.

Income tax in the United Kingdom is highly progressive.

For the large majority of contributors, who are wage and salary earners, income tax is deducted by the employer on behalf of the Inland Revenue. This system is known as the PAYE system (Pay As You Earn). This has the advantage of being economic to operate and efficient.

In 1981–82 income tax receipts totalled £28·5 billion (28% of the total tax burden).

Corporation tax

Corporation tax was introduced in 1965 and is levied on all resident companies, corporate bodies and unincorporated associations, though not partnerships or local authorities. The rate of corporation tax for 1981/82 is 52%. Small companies with profits of less than £80,000 are exempt, and those earning between £80,000 and £200,000 pay a reduced rate.

Petroleum Revenue Tax (PRT)

PRT is charged on profits from the extraction of oil and gas under licence in Britain and from the British sector of the Continental Shelf. The tax was introduced at a rate of 45% in 1974, but this had been raised to 70% by March 1982.

(b) Taxes on capital

Capital Transfer Tax (CTT)

CTT applies to the transfer of personal wealth during a person's lifetime or on death, although transfers during life are charged at a reduced rate. The first £50,000 is exempt from tax, but the rates on the remainder rise from 15% to 75% on the excess over £2·01 million.

Capital Gains Tax (CGT)

CGT is charged on capital gains accruing on the disposal of assets. Private motor cars, the principal private residence and National Savings Certificates are exempt from CGT, which is charged at a rate of 30%. Gains of less than £3,000 during a year are exempt.

Development Land Tax (DLT)

The DLT was introduced in 1976, and is charged at a rate of 60% on realized development values of over £50,000.

(c) Taxes on spending

1. Central government

Taxes on spending levied by central government consist of value added tax, car tax, customs and excise duties, and protective duties – which are collected by the Board of Customs and Excise, and other miscellaneous expenditure taxes such as stamp duties and motor vehicles excise duty.

Value Added Tax (VAT)

VAT was introduced on 1 April 1973 and is a tax on consumption borne by the consumer. VAT is collected at each stage of production and distribution; each trader pays VAT on the value of the goods and services received, and then charges VAT on the value of goods and services supplied. The trader effectively pays only the difference between the output and the input tax to the Customs and Excise, and thus bears no tax.

VAT is charged at a standard rate of 15%, although certain goods are exempt and others such as food and children's clothing are zero rated. Both these mean that the consumer does not pay tax.

2. Local government

The principal local taxes are the 'rates'. Land and buildings are given a rateable value. Depending upon its financial requirements for the coming year the local authority declares a 'rate-poundage', the amount charged to each taxpayer is calculated by multiplying the rateable value by the rate poundage. Thus if a building has a rateable value of £200, and the rate poundage for a given year is 30p, then the ratepayer will be charged £60. The rateable value of properties is reviewed about every five years.

The Budget

Each year the Chancellor of the Exchequer must present a Budget to the House of Commons. A budget is necessary to arrange the raising of tax revenue for the following year, for although many taxes are permanent (unless amended), the taxes on incomes and profits are imposed for only one year at a time. A budget is accompanied by the *'Financial Statement and Budget Report'* which contains a review of the economy over the past year with the prospects for the coming year. However the budget does not simply propose the necessary tax legislation, for the Chancellor also describes the economic policies which the government intends to follow and the changes in government revenues and expenditures which form part of these policies.

Budgetary policy

Since 1945, governments of all political persuasions have attempted to follow economic policies designed to maintain:

1. A high and stable level of employment.
2. A low and stable level of price inflation.
3. A high rate of economic growth.
4. A satisfactory balance of payments.

Different governments have followed very different policies in an attempt to fulfill these aims. However a major problem occurs since in some circumstances the aims conflict, and a policy designed to achieve one of the aims, can at the same time deteriorate the position regarding one of the other aims. It is widely considered that the government should attempt to reach a situation where the overall level of demand in the economy is just sufficient to match the supply of goods and services. If the level of demand is too high, demand-pull inflation may well follow, but if demand is too low, unemployment will result as firms will experience a low demand for their output, and will therefore reduce employment.

If the level of demand in the economy is considered to be just right, the government will introduce a *balanced budget*, where the reduction in demand caused by taxation is exactly matched by the increase in demand caused by government spending on goods and services.

If demand is too low, the government will plan a *budget deficit*; this means that government spending will exceed taxation, and this will increase the level of demand in the economy. The government finances this deficit by borrowing.

If demand is too high, the government will introduce a *budget surplus*; this means that the revenue from taxation will exceed government spending, and this action will reduce the level of demand in the economy.

The Conservative government (1979–) has tended to use demand management techniques far less than previous ones, and therefore budgetary policy is far less important today.

Key terms

'Public goods' are services which have to be provided by the state, because the private sector will be unwilling to do so.

The Principles of taxation are equity, certainty, economy and convenience.

A direct tax is a tax which is levied directly on income, wealth or property.

An indirect tax is a tax levied on goods and services.

The Budget is an estimate of government spending and revenue for the coming year, presented by the Chancellor of the Exchequer. A budget surplus occurs when taxation revenue exceeds government spending, and thus reduces the level of demand in the economy. A budget deficit occurs when the revenue from taxation is exceeded by government spending, increasing the level of demand in the economy.

A balanced budget occurs when the revenue from taxation is equal to government spending.

Chapter 17
International Trade

Specialization not only occurs within a country, but also between countries. Nations concentrate on the production of those goods and services for which they have the greatest advantage over other countries. A proportion of output may then be exchanged for other goods and services produced by other countries. The main reason for studying international trade is to examine why nations engage in trade, what goods are traded and the manner in which trade occurs. The main difference between internal trade and international trade is that countries use different currencies, and therefore before international trade can occur it must be possible to exchange one currency for another. International payments are examined in detail in the next chapter.

The basis of trade

Countries specialize in the production of those goods and services which they are able to produce more cheaply than other countries. A nation may enjoy either a 'natural' or an 'acquired' advantage over other countries, enabling it to produce a particular good or service more cheaply. For example, Jamaica has a 'natural' advantage over the United Kingdom in the production of sugar, that advantage being a more suitable climate. The United Kingdom has a natural advantage over Jamaica in the production of petroleum products, through the resources of oil. An acquired advantage exists where a nation has made developments in the production of a commodity and is able to produce the good more cheaply than other countries. Examples of acquired advantages include 'Swiss watches', and 'Japanese transistor radios'.

The gains from trade

A hypothetical example can illustrate the gains that countries can achieve by specializing in the production of certain goods, and engaging in trade. In the following example it is assumed that there are only two nations, the United Kingdom and Jamaica, and that there are only two commodities, sugar and petroleum products. It is also assumed that barriers to trade do not exist, such as transport costs and tariffs.

Table 36 shows the level of production that the United Kingdom and Jamaica could each attain if they were to concentrate all their economic resources into either the production of sugar or petroleum products (as measured in some common unit of output).

Country	Units of output		
	Sugar		Petroleum products
United Kingdom	4	*OR*	20
Jamaica	18	*OR*	2

Table 36. Production possibilities of the United Kingdom and Jamaica

Without specialization and trade, each nation may decide to allocate one half of its resources to the production of each good. The level of production in each country of each good will be as follows, in Table 37.

Country	Units of output	
	Sugar	Petroleum products
United Kingdom	2	10
Jamaica	9	1
Total production	11	11

Table 37. Production level without specialization

Without specialization the United Kingdom will produce 2 units of sugar and 10 units of petroleum products. Jamaica will produce 9 units of sugar and 1 unit of petroleum products. Total world production will amount to 11 units of sugar and 11 units of petroleum products.

If each nation decides to specialize in that good for which it has an advantage, then Jamaica will devote all her economic resources to sugar production, and the United Kingdom will produce only petroleum products (see Table 38 for levels of production).

Through specialization, total production rises to 18 units of sugar and 20 units of petroleum products, an increase of 7 units of sugar and 9 units of petroleum products. The countries can then trade with each other, and both will obtain an advantage in the form of a higher consumption of both sugar and petroleum products, than was the case before specialization.

Country	Units of output	
	Sugar	Petroleum products
United Kingdom	0	20
Jamaica	18	0
Total production	18	20

Table 38. Production levels with specialization

The limits to trade

In the real world some limits on the gains which accrue from specialization and trade may occur.

1. Transport costs between nations may be so high that they exceed the gains from specialization and trade.
2. Nations may feel the need to have secure supplies of certain products, and will continue to produce certain goods which could be bought at a cheaper price from other countries, in case of a breakdown of supplies caused by, for example, international conflicts.
3. Nations may be unable to obtain the total requirements of a product through trade.

The terms of trade

The rate at which the goods of one country are exchanged for the goods of another is given by the terms of trade. The terms of trade are expressed as follows:

$$\text{Terms of trade} = \frac{\text{Index of export prices}}{\text{Index of import prices}}$$

Year	Exports index	Imports index	Terms of trade
1971	53·9	44·3	121·7
1972	56·9	46·7	121·8
1973	64·0	59·6	107·4
1974	81·7	87·4	93·5
1975	100·0	100·0	100·0
1976	120·7	121·6	99·3
1977	142·4	141·4	100·7

Table 39. U.K. terms of trade 1971 to 1977 (1975 = 100)

If the price of the U.K.'s exports rise faster than the price of imported goods, the terms of trade figure will rise. This is termed an improvement in the terms of trade as fewer British goods will have to be exported to pay for a specific volume of imports. On the other hand, if the price of U.K. imports rise faster than the price of exported goods, the terms of trade figure will fall. This is termed a deterioration in the terms of trade as more British goods will have to be exported to pay for a specific quantity of imports.

An improvement in the terms of trade is not necessarily beneficial to the nation, nor need a deterioration in the terms of trade prove detrimental. For example, if the demand for the U.K.'s exports is elastic, then an improvement in the terms of trade, indicating that a rise has occurred in the price of Britain's exports greater than the rise in the price of foreign goods, then the demand for British goods may fall considerably. A deterioration in the terms of trade can prove beneficial if the demand for the U.K.'s exports is elastic, since the relative fall in the price of exports may induce a large increase in the demand for British exports.

The demand for British exports abroad is, in fact elastic; the demand for foreign imports in the U.K. is inelastic.

Restrictions on trade

Despite the apparent advantages which can be obtained through trade, nations place artificial barriers to restrict trade. The main forms of restriction are:

1. Tariffs

A tariff is a tax on an imported good. There are two basic types of tariff (a) *specific* tariffs, whereby a quantity of a commodity is taxed regardless of its value (e.g. a gallon of whisky, a barrel of oil) and (b) an *ad valorem* tariff, whereby the tax on an imported good is charged at a percentage of the import price. If an imported good is subject to a tariff, then the price of the good in the domestic market will increase, thus reducing the quantity sold, and therefore the volume of imports. A major problem with tariffs is that if a country imposes a tariff on the imports of a good from another country, that country may retaliate by imposing tariffs on its own imports. If this occurs then the volume of trade will be further reduced.

2. Quotas

A quota is a quantitative restriction on the imports of a good, or on the volume of imports from a particular nation. For example, a nation may impose a quota of 10,000 motor cars per month, regardless of their origin, or it may impose a quota of 10,000 cars per month from Japan.

3. Exchange controls

A nation can place restrictions on trade through a system of exchange controls. To buy imports from a foreign country, an importer requires foreign currency. If the government places controls on the amount of foreign currency which importers can buy, then the volume of imports will be reduced. The government can, for example, refuse to supply foreign currencies for the importation of certain products.

4. Subsidies

Governments often provide subsidies for firms and nationalized industries, and this will affect the volume of trade. For example, a subsidy to a textile manufacturer by the British government will enable the firm to lower its price and this will reduce the volume of imports of textiles. Countries sometimes subsidize exports to increase their volume of sales abroad.

Arguments for Protection

The main reason for a nation placing restrictions on its trade with other nations is to protect its own interests, and the main arguments in favour of this type of activity are listed below:

1. To raise revenue At one time revenue from duties on imported goods was an important source of government revenue. But protective duties form only a small part of government revenue today.

2. To protect declining industries Some domestic industries may require protection from overseas competition to ensure a managed contraction, otherwise large-scale unemployment may result, and this will be particularly serious where an industry is highly localized. For example, the British cotton industry has been protected against cheap imports both by the use of tariffs and quotas.

3. To protect infant industries Some industries require protection from foreign competition during their formative years, while their costs (and thus their prices) remain high, until they are able to achieve the economies of scale, which they will be unable to attain until their production reaches a certain level, which may not occur for a few years.

4. Security of supplies A nation may protect an industry to ensure that the domestic production of a good is continued to ensure the secure supplies of that good for future years.

5. To aid the balance of payments Protection may be used to aid the balance of payments by reducing the volume of imports.

6. To reduce general unemployment A nation may be successful in reducing general unemployment by placing restrictions on the importation of foreign goods. Consumers will have to buy home produced goods, and thus firms will employ more workers to cope with this increase in demand. A problem with this action is that the introduction of protective duties will encourage retaliation from other countries which may then reduce exports, and total demand for British goods may therefore remain unchanged.

GATT

The General Agreement on Tariffs and Trade (GATT) was first established in 1947, when 23 countries agreed to pursue policies which would encourage trade between nations, by reducing the barriers to trade which existed, particularly tariffs, quantitative import quotas, subsidies on exports and preferential trading agreements. There are now 76 members of GATT, and there has been some success since 1947 in reducing trade barriers. The most notable achievement of the member nations was to reduce tariffs by over 35 % in the mid 1960s during the Kennedy Round of talks (1964–1967). Further progress was made during the Tokyo Round (1973–79).

Britain's overseas trade

In 1980 Britain was the fifth largest trading nation in the world. Exports of goods were valued at £47,389 million, and imports were valued at £46,211 million.
Britain's overseas trade can be analysed in two ways. Firstly by a study of the composition of imports and exports, and secondly by an examination of the geographical distribution of imports and exports.

The composition of trade

The composition of trade by commodity is given in Figure 28.
The most notable changes in the composition of Britain's exports since 1955 have been the decline in exports of textiles, basic materials and metals. Although the overall share of manufactures rose between 1955 and 1965, this has since fallen, primarily due to reductions in the export of road vehicles, metals and textiles. However, exports of chemicals and other manufactures have risen throughout this period, and to some extent this has compensated for reductions elsewhere.

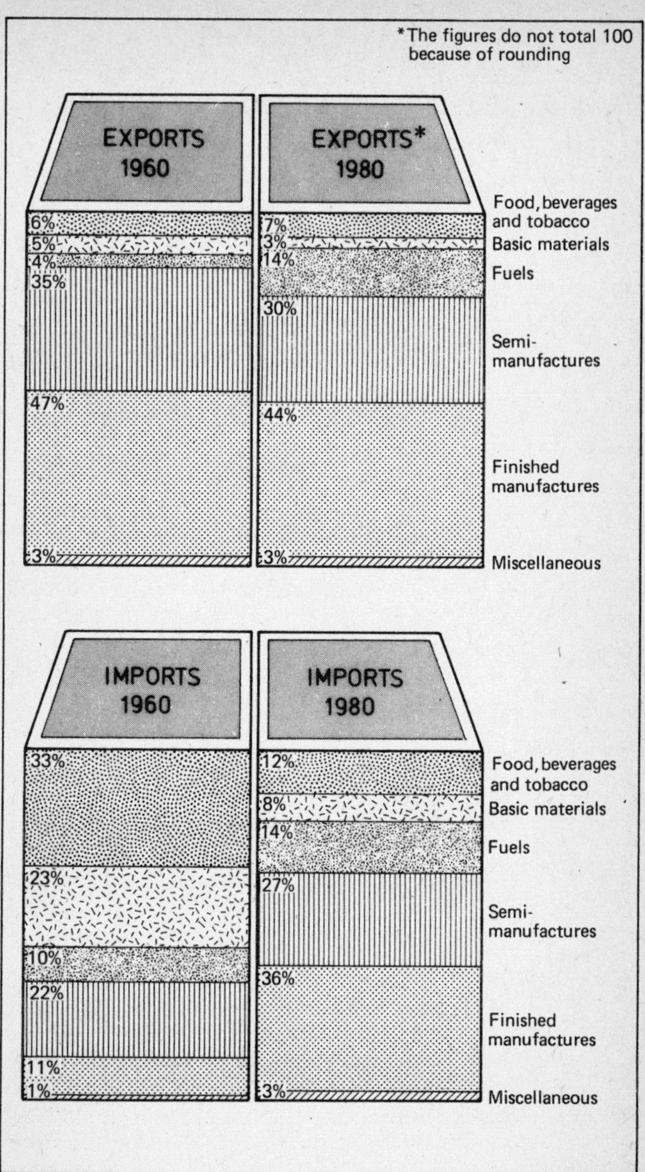

Figure 28. Commodity composition of U.K. Trade (1980)

The geographical distribution of trade

The geographical distribution of Britain's trade is shown in Figure 29.

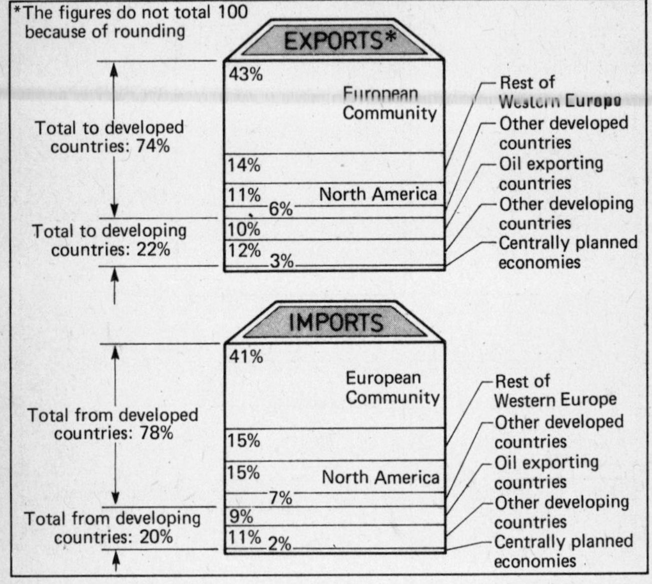

Figure 29. The Geographical Distribution of U.K. Trade 1980

The major changes which have occurred in the geographical distribution of Britain's overseas trade lies in Britain's joining of the EEC, and the quadrupling of the price of oil in 1973/74. Britain's membership of the EEC has had two effects. Other EEC nations have become more important both as a source of supply, and as a destination for British exports. At the same time, the importance of other developed nations has declined (in particular, trade with Canada, Australia and New Zealand). The increase in the price of oil which occurred in 1973/74 increased the earnings of the oil exporting countries, which in turn enabled the U.K. to increase her exports to these nations considerably, and these nations now account for one seventh of all British exports.

The Common Market

On 1 January 1973 Britain, together with the Irish Republic and Denmark joined the original six countries which had formed the European Community. The original six members were Belgium, France, The Federal Republic of Germany, Italy, Luxembourg and the Netherlands.

The European Community consists of three communities set up by separate treaties, the *European Coal and Steel Community* (ECSC), the *European Economic Community* (EEC), and the *European Atomic Energy Commission* (Euratom).

The ECSC was set up in 1952 to establish a common market for coal and steel, it abolished duties and restrictions on trade in coal and steel between members. It has encouraged the use of mechanization and modernization, and has provided funds to workers laid off by pit closures.

Euratom was established in 1957 to coordinate the peaceful development of nuclear power in member nations.

The EEC was formed in 1957 with the aim of establishing economic unity between member nations.

The separate institutions established by the three communities were merged in 1967.

The EEC

The objectives of the EEC as laid out in the Treaty of Rome were as follows:

1. The creation of a customs union, the abolition of internal tariffs and other barriers to trade and the establishment of a common external tariff.
2. The development of a common policy for agriculture.
3. The introduction of measures designed to establish the free movement of labour, capital and services.
4. The provision of preferential treatment for overseas countries which had special links with member countries.

There are four main institutions which are responsible for the running of the community. These institutions are the Council of Ministers, the European Commission, the European Court of Justice and the European Parliament.

The Council of Ministers consists of one minister from each member state, and a representative of the Commission, and has to approve any major decision. The Council meets as a Council of Foreign Ministers, a Council of Agricultural Ministers, of Industry Ministers, and so on. A Council of Heads of Government meets three times a year.

The Commission is the civil service of the community, which numbers about 8,000. It is headed by 13 Commissioners, who are appointed for a period of four years. It is the Commission which implements the decisions of the Council of Ministers.

The Court of Justice deals with cases of community law, and consists of 11 judges.

The Parliament is directly elected by the voters of member states. France, Germany, Italy and the U.K. each have 81 seats in the Parliament, the Netherlands has 25 seats, Belgium has 24, Denmark 16, Ireland 15 and Luxembourg 6.

Key terms

The terms of trade are expressed as the ratio of the index of export prices over the index of import prices.

A tariff is a tax on an imported good.

A quota is a quantatative restriction on the volume of a commodity imported.

GATT (the General Agreement on Tariffs and Trade) is an organization which attempts to encourage the growth of international trade by reducing the barriers to trade.

The European Community consists of the European Economic Community (EEC), the European Coal and Steel Community (ECSC), and the European Atomic Energy Commission (Euratom).

Chapter 18
International Payments

The main difference between internal trade and international trade is that different countries use different currencies. Foreign imports into Britain will have to be paid for in foreign currencies, and will involve an outflow of funds. British exports to foreign countries are paid for in sterling, and involve a flow of funds into the United Kingdom. It is therefore of the utmost importance that British importers can exchange sterling for foreign currencies, and that importers of British goods in foreign countries can exchange their currencies for sterling.

The balance of payments

The balance of payments is a table which shows the financial transactions of the U.K. with the rest of the world. It is important to remember that if a good is imported into the U.K., then an outflow of funds will occur to pay for this good, whereas an export of goods will be followed by an inflow of funds. The United Kingdom Balance of Payments for 1980 is shown in Table 39; it is organized into four main sections.

1. The current balance

The current balance is obtained by the summation of the visible balance and the invisible balance.

Visible trade

Trade in goods, such as manufactures, food and raw materials is termed visible trade, and in 1980 the U.K. had a balance of trade surplus of £1,178 million. Traditionally the value of goods imported into the U.K. has exceeded the value of goods exported. However, in 1980 Britain enjoyed a substantial improvement in visible trade, resulting in the first trade surplus since 1971.

Invisible trade

Trade in services, such as shipping, civil aviation, travel, wages and salaries, profits and dividends is termed invisible trade. Britain has consistently earned a surplus on invisible transactions which has often exceeded the deficit on visible trade. In fact, earnings of foreign currency from tourism alone, exceeds the foreign currency earnings of North Sea oil.

The balance of transactions on visible trade and invisible trade (i.e. trade in goods and services) gives the current balance.

	£ million
Visible trade	
Exports	47,389
Imports	46,211
Visible balance	+1,178
Invisible trade	
Credits	25,764
Debits	23,736
Invisible balance	+2,028
1. Current balance	+3,206
2. Investment and other capital flows	−1,475
3. Balancing item	−539
Total currency flow (1+2+3)	+1,192
4. Official financing	
Transactions with IMF and overseas monetary authorities	+40
Foreign currency borrowing	−941
Drawing on (+)/additions to (−) official reserves	−291
Total official financing	−1,192

Table 40. The U.K. balance of payments (1980)

2. Investment and other capital flows

Investment in foreign countries by British residents represents an outflow of funds and requires an exchange of currency. Similarly, foreign residents invest in the U.K., and this represents an inflow of funds. Capital movements of this type are recorded under the heading '*investment and other capital flows*'. In 1977 the combined effect of all capital flows was an inflow of £4,410 million.

3. The balancing item

The balancing item is the net effect of omissions and errors (mainly the under-recording of some transactions) in the capital account. In 1980 this figure was −£539 million.

4. The total currency flow

The summation of the current account, investment and other capital flows and the balancing item gives the total currency flow. A positive figure indicates that there has been a net inflow of funds, whereas a negative figure indicates that there has been a net outflow of funds. In 1980 there was a net inflow of £1,192 million.

Official financing

The total currency flow has to be financed by the central government. An outflow of funds would necessitate a reduction in the nation's reserves of foreign currency, or would have to be financed by borrowing either from other nations or the International Monetary Fund (IMF). In 1980, the nation lent out £901 million in foreign currency, and with a total currency inflow of £1,192 million, this meant that the nation's reserves were increased by a total of £291 million.

In this way the balance of payments always balances, since any outflows are financed by a reduction in the nations reserves of foreign currency, whereas an inflow of funds adds to the nations reserves.

Exchange rates

A rate of exchange is the price of one currency in terms of another. The need to exchange currencies lies in international trade. Currencies are traded on the foreign exchange market, and the rate at which one currency exchanges for another is determined by the interaction of the demand for and the supply of each currency. If the demand for a currency exceeds the supply, then the price of that currency (the exchange rate) will rise. If the supply of a currency exceeds demand, then the price of the currency will fall. The supply of and the demand for a currency originate in trading and investment. If a British firm imports French cars, then the firm will demand French francs and supply sterling to the foreign exchange market (since the French firm will require payment in francs and not in pounds sterling). Similarly, if a British firm builds a factory in Canada, it will demand Canadian dollars and will supply sterling.
Therefore if the value of British imports plus British investment overseas exceeds the value of British exports plus overseas investment in the U.K., then the supply of sterling will exceed the demand for sterling and the price of sterling will fall. If exports exceed imports, then the exchange rate will rise.

Floating exchange rates

If an exchange rate is allowed to find its own value in the foreign exchange market, without any government interference, it is described as a freely fluctuating or floating exchange rate. The floating exchange rate system is claimed to have a self-regulating relationship with the balance of payments.

If a nation experiences an outflow of foreign currency (this can be determined by an examination of the balance of payments), then the supply of that nation's currency on the foreign exchange market will exceed demand, and its rate of exchange will fall. This will raise the price of its imports, and reduce the price of its exports. Imports will fall, exports will rise; the demand for the currency will increase and the supply of the currency will fall. This will bring about an equilibrium position where the demand and supply are equal, and the exchange rate will stabilize. If the demand for a currency exceeds supply, the price of the currency will rise, making exports more expensive and imports cheaper. Thus imports will increase, exports will fall, and at the higher exchange rate the demand for and the supply of the currency will be equal.

The major problem associated with floating exchange rates is that the rate may be unstable, and this will discourage firms from engaging in international trade, and some countries will therefore be unable to achieve the gains that can be made from trade. Floating exchange rates operated in the 1930s, and also in the 1970s, although governments do intervene in foreign exchange markets to ensure exchange rates remain relatively stable.

Fixed exchange rates

A system of fixed exchange rates was introduced after the Second World War. Currencies were expressed in terms of the American dollar, and the rate of exchange was termed the currency's 'par-value'. Currencies were allowed to vary within limits of 1% either side of the par value, and governments were responsible for ensuring that the rate did not vary by a greater amount. If the demand for a currency exceeded supply, and there was a pressure for the exchange rate to fall, then the government would artificially raise demand by buying its own currency and selling foreign currency. If supply was exceeded by demand the government would sell its own currency and buy foreign currencies. The major problem with this system was that nations with balance of payments difficulties (where imports exceeded exports) had to use resources to buy its own currency, but did not allow the value of the currency to fall, with the result that some nations continually suffered from low exports and high imports.

The system allowed nations to devalue or revalue their currency, but this could only be done once it was clear that the currency was either overvalued or undervalued, and for those nations which had an overvalued currency, the loss of their foreign currency reserves might have already been massive. The system of fixed exchange rates was abandoned in 1971.

The International Monetary Fund

The Bretton Woods agreement of 1944 established the World Bank and the International Monetary Fund (IMF). The World Bank was set up to promote long-term development in the developing countries by providing funds for capital projects, such as dams and power stations, at subsidized rates of interest. The IMF became the central organisation of the world's monetary system, and began its operations in 1947. The major purpose of the IMF was to promote the expansion of international trade through a system of fixed exchange rates, and by providing short-term assistance for nations with temporary balance of payments difficulties, in the form of loans and specialist advice, thus enabling countries to support the exchange rate of their currency. If a country experienced a persistent disequilibrium in its balance of payments, the Fund had to be consulted before devaluation could proceed to ensure a round of competitive devaluations did not occur.

Currencies were fixed in terms of the American dollar, and member nations were responsible for ensuring that the exchange rate varied by no more than 1% from the par value. However the weakness of the dollar and the rigidity of the system created some major problems, and the Bretton Woods system broke down in 1971. The IMF, set up as the central cog of the Bretton Woods system did not disappear. Although the system of fixed exchange rates failed, the need for stable exchange rates was appreciated, and nowadays the main purpose of the IMF is to encourage the growth of world trade through a system of stable exchange rates. The IMF continues to provide assistance for nations with balance of payments and exchange rate difficulties. For example the U.K. was provided with massive loans during 1976 and 1977.

Today the IMF has 138 members, and governments pay a quota which is dependant on the size of their economy, and their contribution to world trade. The size of each country's quota is expressed in Special Drawing Rights (SDR's), and at present exchange rates 1 SDR=1 dollar (American). The United States' quota is 8·4 billion SDRs, the U.K.'s quota is 2·9 billion SDRs, and West Germany's is 2·1 billion SDRs. Nations pay quotas in their own currency (75%), and in foreign currencies (25%). A nation may withdraw up to 25% of its quota under certain circumstances, and further withdrawals are allowed, but these are usually accompanied by conditions which force the acceptance of advice on economic policies. The loans which the U.K. managed to obtain in the mid 1970s were accompanied by conditions which forced the government to reduce government spending and increase taxation.

Key terms

The balance of payments is a table which shows the financial transactions of the U.K. with the rest of the world.
Visible trade consists of trade in goods.
Invisible trade consists of trade in services.
The current balance is the balance of transactions on visible and invisible trade.
The balancing item is the net effect of omissions and errors in the capital account of the balance of payments.
The total currency flow provides the net effect of international trade on the nation's funds of foreign reserves, once transactions with the IMF, and foreign currency borrowings have been added.
A rate of exchange is the price of one currency in terms of another.
An exchange rate is described as **freely fluctuating** if it is allowed to find its own value in the foreign exchange market.
The International Monetary Fund was established by the Bretton Woods agreement of 1944 to promote the expansion of world trade.

Index

Examination Hints

How to study economics

Clearly a knowledge of how to study economics is important to every student who wishes to succeed in economics examinations. There are two basic aspects of most courses in economics:

1. Description The student requires a good basic knowledge of the British economy, and a broad understanding of the international economy. It is very important that the student is acquainted with up-to-date information, and publications such as The Economist, Social Trends, and The Annual Abstract of Statistics are very useful in keeping knowledge up-to-date.

2. Theory The basic theoretical aspects must be known thoroughly, especially the theory relating to the price system and to the costs of production. Several self-testing workbooks are now available, and these are extremely useful when studying the theoretical aspects of the course.

Method

This examination hints section contains a list of essay questions taken from past GCE O-level papers in economics, and these are similar to those questions you will meet in the examination. After studying a topic, try to answer a relevant essay question. You can then pick out some questions from past examination papers. By following this method, you will gain experience in the type of question you will meet in your own examination.

Writing essays

Many students who have a good grasp of the subject are unable to communicate their knowledge to the examiner as they are unable to express their knowledge in essay-form. This is due to a poor essay-writing technique. There are some general rules which will aid you in writing essays.

1. **Read the question thoroughly** Many students attempt to answer a question because they see a particular word in the title e.g. population, and this is a topic which they have studied in depth; frequently, they realize too late that the essay is really about something totally unrelated to the topic 'population'.

2. **Form an essay plan** You MUST ALWAYS form an essay

plan. This ensures the essay follows a logical pattern, and is not just a series of facts. An essay plan must always contain an introduction, this is the opportunity for giving any definitions, and for introducing the subject. The essay should always include a conclusion when you draw together all information that has been included in the main part of the text. It is often useful to include the exact wording of the title in the conclusion, this will encourage you to make the essay more relevant. An essay plan for the following question might be as follows: What are the main advantages and disadvantages of the mixed economy?

1, Introduction – what is a mixed economy.
2. Advantages of the mixed economy.
3. Disadvantages of the mixed economy.
4, Conclusion.

3. **Use simple language** Do not try to use long sentences. Keep them short and concise.
4. **Be neat and tidy** Many examination boards ask their examiners to penalise work which is untidy and/or careless. Make sure that you do not lose marks for this reason.
5. **Keep to the point** Many students tend to wander off the subject, and lose marks. Keep to your essay plan and do not allow yourself to wander off the subject.
6. **Answer the question** Many students provide some very good answers, but not to the question they are answering. Always make sure that you are answering the question.

Bibliography

It is important that you use good textbooks whilst studying economics. Some highly respected textbooks which are designed for GCE O-level and CSE students are given below.

Starting Economics F. Davies
Daily Economics J. Nobbs and P. Ames
Economics: An Introductory Course D. Baron
Essential Economics Sapsford and Ladd
Economics in Action D. Christie and A. Scott
Descriptive Economics (+ workbook) C. D. Harbury
Elementary Economics (+ workbook) J. Harvey
Economic Society K. Marder and L. Alderson

This list of textbooks is organized in an order of difficulty, thus the first few books are most suitable for CSE, whereas those towards the end are more suited for the O-level candidate.

Examination questions

Some examination questions from past papers are provided below. Questions are listed on a chapter to chapter basis.

Chapter 1.

What are the main advantages and disadvantages of the mixed economy?

Distinguish between capital goods and consumer goods. What is the importance of this distinction? (Welsh)

Chapter 2

Why are workers often reluctant to change jobs? What effect does this have on employment in different regions of the U.K.? (AEB)

What are the main causes of unemployment? Suggest remedies for any one of them. (Oxford)

Chapter 3

In spite of the general trend to large-scale units the small firm continues to survive in the United Kingdom. Why is this so? Give examples of some industries in which the small firm plays an important part. (AEB)

Explain what is meant by economies of scale. Distinguish between internal and external economies. (Oxford)

Chapter 4

What is meant by optimum size of a firm? What disadvantages arise if a firm expanded beyond its optimum size? (Oxford)

The following figures refer to the output and total cost of a manufactured commodity:

Output	Total cost (£)
0	100
1	120
2	134
3	144
4	152

(a) What are the fixed costs?

(b) (i) What is average cost when total cost is £152?

(ii) what is the marginal cost of the third unit?

(AEB)

Chapter 5

What is the principle of limited liability? What are its advantages to (a) investors and (b) firms? (AEB)

What are the main differences between joint-stock companies and nationalized industries? (Oxford)

Chapter 6
Describe and briefly comment upon the economic functions of the retailer. (Welsh)
How and why has the organization of retailing changed in Britain since 1945? (Oxford and Cambridge)
Chapter 7
What factors determine the location of industry in Britain? (Oxford)
Explain why it is that some industries are highly localized while others are scattered throughout the country? (Oxford)
Chapter 8
Describe and account for the existing geographical distribution of Britain's working population. (AEB)
The recent (1971) Census of Population showed that between 1961 and 1971 the population of the U.K. rose by nearly 3 million. What were the causes of this increase? What are some of the likely consequences? (AEB)
For what reasons may the size of a country's population change? (Southern)
Chapter 9
What does the economist mean by demand? What are the principal factors affecting the demand for refrigerators? (AEB)
What do economists mean by 'a market'? What conditions in a market lead to (a) rising prices, and (b) falling prices? (Welsh)
Chapter 10
What is a monopoly? Are there any reasons why monopolies should be subject to state control? (Oxford)
Chapter 11
Distinguish between a craft union and a general trade union. What benefits can a worker expect from joining a trade union? (AEB)
Why do architects earn more than building labourers? (Welsh)
Chapter 12
What is a cheque? What are the advantages of using a cheque? Assess the importance of the cheque as a means of payment in the United Kingdom at the present time. (Welsh)
What is meant by the statement: 'Money is a medium of exchange'? How far do you consider this to be a satisfactory definition of money? (AEB)
Chapter 13
Explain how the Index of Retail prices is constructed. What problems are there in constructing such an index?
What is meant by inflation?
Discuss its possible effects.

Chapter 14
Outline the main elements of the capital market, and discuss their functions.
How can the Bank of England control and influence commercial banks?
Chapter 15
Explain how the national income of a country is calculated. Why is it important to know the size of the national income?(Oxford)
What is meant by national income? What factors determine its growth? (Southern)
Chapter 16
Give two examples of indirect taxes. What are the advantages of (a) direct and (b) indirect taxation? (AEB)
What are the main purposes of government expenditure? (adapted)
Chapter 17
Describe the pattern of foreign trade of the U.K. at the present time with regard to the main types of imports and exports, and their geographical distribution. (AEB)
What are the purposes of international trade? (Southern)
Chapter 18
What are the main items in a country's balance of payments? Explain how a country's ability to lend abroad is dependent on its balance of payments on current account. (Oxford)
Distinguish between fixed and floating exchange rates. Comment on the advantages and disadvantages of each.

Examination Papers

Syllabuses and booklets of past examination questions can be obtained from bookshops and from the relevant examining board. The GCE and CSE Examining Boards are listed below, together with their addresses.

GCE Examining Boards

University of Cambridge Local Examinations Syndicate
The Secretary, Syndicate Buildings, 17 Harvey Road, Cambridge.
Southern Universities' Joint Board for Schools Examinations
The Secretary, Cotham Road, Bristol BS6 6DD.
Joint Matriculation Board
The Secretary, Joint Matriculation Board, Manchester M15 6EU.
University of London School Examination Council
The Secretary, 66–72 Gower Street, London WC1E 6EE.
Oxford and Cambridge Schools Examination Board
The Secretary, 10 Trumpington St, Cambridge CB2 1QE and Elsfield Way, Oxford OX2 8EP.
Oxford Delegacy of Local Examinations
The Secretary, Oxford Local Examinations, Ewert Place, Summertown, Oxford OX2 7BZ.
Welsh Joint Education Committee
The Secretary, 245 Western Ave., Cardiff CF5 2YX.
Associated Examining Board for the GCE
The Secretary, Wellington House, Station Road, Aldershot, Hants GU11 1BQ.
Northern Ireland Schools Examinations Council
The Secretary, Beechill House, 42 Beechill Road,
Belfast BT6 4RS.

CSE Regional Examining Boards

East Anglian Regional Examinations Board
'The Lindens', Lexden Road, Colchester, Essex CO3 3RL.
East Midland Regional Examinations Board
Robins Wood House, Robins Wood Road, Apsley, Nottingham NG8 3NH.
Associated Lancashire Schools Examining Board
77, Whitworth St., Manchester M1 6HA.
Metropolitan Regional Examinations Board
Lyon House, 104 Wandsworth High St., London SW18 4LF.

Middlesex Regional Examining Board
56–63 Wembley Hill Road, Wembley, Middlesex HA9 8BH.
North Regional Examinations Board
Wheatfield Road, Westerhope, Newcastle upon Tyne NE5 5JZ.
North Western Secondary Schools Examinations Board
Orbit House, Albert Street, Eccles, Manchester M30 0WL.
Northern Ireland Schools Examination Council
Beechill House, Beechill Road, Belfast BT6 4RS.
Southern Regional Examinations Board
58 London Road, Southampton SO9 4YL.
The South-East Regional Examinations Board
Beloe House, 2–4 Mount Ephraim Road, Tunbridge Wells, Kent TN1 1EU.
South Western Examinations Board
23–29 Marsh Street, Bristol BS1 4NJ.
Welsh Joint Education Committee (CSE Examinations Sub-Committee), 245 Western Ave., Cardiff CF5 2YX
West Midlands Examinations Board
Norfolk House, Smallbrook, Queensway, Birmingham B5 4NJ.
West Yorkshire and Lindsey Regional Examining Board
Scardale House, 136 Derbyshire Lane, Sheffield S8 8SE.
Yorkshire Regional Examinations Board
31–33 Springfield Ave., Harrogate, Yorks, HG1 2HR.

Key Facts Revision Section

Chapter 1. Introducing economics

Economics is the study of how man uses economic resources to produce goods and services so as to satisfy his needs and wants.

The economic problem

A community's economic resources consist of natural resources (land and raw materials), capital goods and labour. A community will have certain needs and demands which will have to be satisfied, and the demand for goods and services will almost certainly exceed the community's ability to produce. This situation is referred to as the economic problem. And a society faced by the basic economic problem must therefore indulge in the process of choosing which demands to fulfil, and which will have to go unsatisfied. In making a choice between competing demands, a production decision is being made. The five production decisions are: What to produce? How much to produce? How to produce? For whom to produce? Where to produce? The problem of choice can be illustrated by the use of a production possibility curve.

Opportunity cost

Opportunity cost is the cost of something in terms of the value of the alternatives which have to be foregone to obtain it.

Economic systems

A community has several important decisions to make about its production and will have to formulate a method to establish how the decisions are going to be made. In theory there are two basic systems. The market economy and the planned economy. However, most countries fall under the heading of the mixed economy.

The market economy

In the market economy resources are privately owned and production decisions are made by private individuals and private firms acting in their own self-interest, in response to the forces of supply and demand. The advantages of the market economy are: (1) Private individuals have the economic freedom to buy and sell as they wish. (2) There is no need for government bureaucracy and red tape. (3) Competiton between firms will encourage low prices, economic efficiency and the invention of new products. (4) Personal rewards for effort and initiative. (5) Only goods required will be produced.

The disadvantages of the market economy are: (1) An unequal distribution of income. (2) Sellers tend to combine into monopolies to enable them to keep prices high and/or keep wages low. (3) Wasteful competition may occur in certain markets. (4) External costs and benefits will not be taken into account. (5) Public goods will not be produced.

The planned economy

In the planned economy production decisions are made by the state planning authorities, guided by social preferences. The main advantages of the planned economy are: (1) Goods can be produced on the basis of need rather than effective demand. (2) The state can plan spending to ensure that the productive capacity of the nation increases. (3) The state can ensure that everyone is employed. (4) No wasteful competition.
The main disadvantages of the planned economy are: (1) Planners may be inefficient. (2) To build up the country's productive potential planners may unduly depress the current standard of living. (3) Planners are less likely to take the risks involved with the introduction of new products. (4) Personal freedom may be reduced if state planning becomes too detailed.

The mixed economy

Many countries have mixed economies. This system attempts to obtain the benefits of both the market and the planned economy, and the disadvantages of neither. There is considerable government interference in what is basically a market economy. The main areas of government activity in the mixed economy are: (1) The provision of public goods. (2) The provision of social welfare schemes. (3) The supervision of private industry to prevent unfair trade practices. (4) The production of goods and services which private industry is unwilling to supply. (5) The overall control of the economy.

Chapter 2. Factors of production

Production

In economics, production refers to the process of fulfilling wants, and all those who are involved in satisfying economic wants are productive. The output of goods and services can be classified into three groups. (1) **Consumer goods,** which consist of **non durable** consumer goods, which have a relatively short life or are consumed in the act of being used and **durable** consumer goods which have a much longer life. (2) **Capital goods,** which aid in the production of other goods and are used by producers. (3) **Ser-**

vices, which are mainly intangible things often consumed at the same time as they are produced.

Factors of production

All productive processes require economic resources before they can proceed, these resources are called factors of production and are classified under the four headings of Land, Labour, Capital and Enterprise. It is sometimes difficult to classify some things under one of these headings.

Land

Land is the term used to describe all natural resources available to man which are the gifts of nature. Some natural resources can be increased in quantity by the application of the other factors of production. However, many natural resources are limited in supply.

The mobility of land

Land is geographically immobile, but land is generally mobile in the sense that it is capable of more than one use.

The law of diminishing returns

As additional units of a variable factor are used with a fixed factor, a point will be reached when the returns derived from the variable factor will decline. Originally, the law of diminishing returns was considered to be specially relevant to land, but it can apply to all the factors of production.

Labour

Labour consists of the human resources which are available to take part in production. A nation's total supply of labour is that proportion of the population who are able and available for work, defined as the working population. The size of the working population is determined by the proportion of the population who are in the working-age group (men 16 to 65, women 16 to 60).

The efficiency of labour

A nation's ability to produce goods and services is not only limited by the supply of labour but also the quality of the labour available.

Education and skill. It is generally believed that higher levels of production are attainable with a skilled, well educated workforce.

Health and welfare. A more healthy workforce will be a more efficient one.

Working conditions. Poor conditions lead to low productivity.

Motivation. The motivation of labour will affect its efficiency. In an attempt to increase workers' motivation, some firms have bonus payments and profit sharing schemes.

The mobility of labour

Labour tends to be both occupationally and geographically immobile. The occupational immobility of labour leads to problems for firms, who experience a shortage of workers with certain skills, and for workers who are unable to obtain employment. The main causes of occupational immobility are: (1) A lack of inherent skill and intelligence. (2) The cost and length of training. (3) Discrimination. (4) Ignorance. (5) Restrictive practices.

Labour is also geographically immobile, and this causes labour shortages in some areas of the country. The main causes of geographical immobility are: (1) The cost of moving home. (2) The cost and availability of housing. (3) Social ties. (4) Family ties. (5) Ignorance of opportunities. (6) Prejudice against living in certain parts of the country.

The division of labour

Man can specialize in the production of those goods for which he has the greatest aptitude. The specialization of labour is termed the division of labour. In a modern society specialization is practised to an extreme degree. The division of labour has certain advantages: (1) Large increases in the productivity of labour. (2) Each man can do the job for which he has the greatest aptitude. (3) Practice makes perfect. (4) The time and cost of training is reduced. (5) Fewer tools are required. (6) Workers do not have to switch operations, and thus time is saved.

The disadvantages of the division of labour are: (1) The continuous repetition of a single task is very monotonous. (2) Loss of craftsmanship. (3) An increased risk of unemployment. (4) Interdependence is increased.

Unemployment

In January 1982 about three million people were in search of a job. A major task of government since the end of the war has been to maintain full employment. The main types of unemployment are: (1) **Frictional unemployment.** A short period of unemployment is often involved when individuals change their jobs. (2) **Seasonal unemployment.** Some areas and occupations suffer from seasonal changes in employment. (3) **Structural unemployment.** This refers to the unemployment which occurs when major industries fall into decline. (4) **Widespread deficiency of demand** can cause general unemployment. The government has attempted to combat unemployment created by a deficiency in demand through its own spending.

Capital
In economics, capital normally refers to capital goods, but capital is a comprehensive term and can cover various types of capital.

Fixed capital consists of assets such as buildings and factories, and is used to produce other goods. **Circulating capital** comprises commodities such as raw materials, which change their appearance in the productive process.
Social capital refers to capital which does not directly take part in production, such as homes, schools and roads.
Capital accumulation. Productive potential can be increased by accumulating capital. If a nation wishes to accumulate capital goods it must do so at the expense of consumer goods and services. Production of new capital is called **investment.**
Capital consumption. During the productive process fixed capital is used up and this is referred to as capital consumption or depreciation.
The mobility of capital. Capital is geographically and occupationally mobile, although some fixed capital is highly immobile in both senses.
Enterprise
The task of combining the factors of production to produce goods and services is performed by the entrepreneur, and is termed enterprise. The entrepreneur takes the financial risk that the business involves, and is responsible for making the decisions about production. In the past these functions were carried out by one person, but as firms have become larger it has increasingly been the case that the two functions have been performed by different groups. The organization of production is performed by skilled managers, and the risk bearing function is carried out by shareholders.

Chapter 3. The Scale of Production

Large firms are now responsible for the lion's share of the nation's output. As firms expand they often enjoy economies of scale. That is, as output expands the cost per unit falls. A diseconomy of scale exists where unit costs increase as output expands.
The optimum size of output is that level of production where the unit costs are lowest.

Economies of scale
(a) Internal economies of scale are those factors which reduce average costs as output expands, they can be classified as follows:

(1) Technical economies, which include specialization, the indivisibility of factors, economies of increased dimensions and the principle of multiples. (2) Managerial economies are those cost advantages that a large firm can enjoy by employing specialist managers. (3) Commercial economies are those cost advantages that the large firm is able to achieve by buying its raw materials, and other factors in bulk. (4) Financial economies arise as it is far easier for a large firm to obtain loan capital, often at lower interest rates than the small firm.

(b) External economies of scale are those reductions in unit costs that are the result of an increase in the size of the industry, or other factors external to the firm. The main external economies are: (1) Economies of information, services and research. (2) Commercial economies. (3) Labour economies. (4) Economies of disintegration.

Diseconomies of scale

Diseconomies of scale are increases in unit costs and can be (a) internal, if they are created within the firm and (b) external, if the cost increases originate outside the firm. The main internal diseconomies are caused by poor communications within large firms, a lack of motivation by workers, poor control by management of the large firm. The main external economies of scale are also called diseconomies of concentration, for they originate when an industry becomes too concentrated in one area. Roads may become congested, housing may be of poor quality, pollution may exist, and there is a danger that the whole area will become depressed if the industry declines.

The growth of the firm

Firms grow so as to achieve higher profits. Firms can either grow in size through internal growth (i.e. using the economies of scale), or through integration (i.e. joining with another firm).

Integration

The main motives for integration are: (1) A greater share of the market. (2) Greater monopoly power over suppliers and buyers. (3) Rationalization of production. (4) An integrated research programme. (5) A more diversified range of products. (6) The sale, or better use of the assets of one of the firms. (7) Access to new markets. (8) Greater availability to economies of scale.

There are three types of integration, (i) horizontal integration occurs when firms combine which operate at the same stage of the productive process, (ii) vertical integration occurs when firms combine which produce at different stages of production and (iii) conglomerate integration occurs when firms combine which produce an unrelated, or only slightly related output.

The small firm

Small firms continue to operate despite the tendency for the average size of the firm to increase. The major reasons for the continued existence of the small firm are: (1) The small firm can provide a personal service to their customers. (2) Many small firms produce an individualized output, for which there is only a small demand. (3) High transport costs will reduce the potential market for each firm and will keep the size of the firm small. (4) Some luxury goods will have only a small demand. (5) A disintegrated industry will keep small firms in operation. (6) Co-operation between small firms enables them to obtain economies of scale. (7) Small firms will continue to exist while some people have a desire to own their own business.

Chapter 4. The Costs of Production

Costs are classified under the following headings:
(1) **Fixed costs** are sometimes referred to as overheads, and consist of rent, rates, depreciation, interest on loans. Fixed costs do not vary with output.
(2) **Variable costs** are those expenses which vary with output. The main variable costs are labour, power and raw materials.
(3) **Total cost** is the addition of fixed and variable costs.
(4) **Average cost** is also known as cost per unit, and is obtained by dividing total cost by units of output.
(5) **Marginal cost** is the cost of an extra unit of output.
(6) **Normal profit** is the cost which must be paid to ensure that the firm continues in the same line of business. Normal profit is a cost to the firm because if the entrepreneur does not earn normal profit, then in the long-run the firm will cease production.

Chapter 5. Business Organization

The three million business organizations in the U.K. are classified under three main headings, Private enterprise, Co-operative enterprise and Public enterprise.

Private enterprise

Private enterprise is further subdivided.
1. **The one-man business** is a firm owned and invariably run by a

single person. The main advantages of the one-man business is that the owner retains personal control and receives personal rewards for initiative and effort. However, such businesses often suffer from a lack of capital, and do not enjoy the advantage of limited liability, they also tend to suffer from a lack of continuity.

2. **The partnership** is a voluntary combination of between 2 and 20 persons, who jointly provide the firm's capital and share the profits. The main advantages of the partnership are that more capital is available, and that partners can specialize; decision making remains flexible. The main disadvantages are that the firm may still suffer from a lack of capital and a lack of continuity, and does not enjoy the advantage of limited liability.

3. **The joint-stock company** is a firm where the capital is raised by the sale of shares to the public and where any profits are distributed to shareholders. Companies are a legal entity in themselves, and shareholders enjoy limited liability, which means that if the firm goes bankrupt holders of shares are only liable for that amount invested in the firm. There are two types of joint-stock company, the private company and the public company.

Private companies must have between 2 and 50 shareholders, but shares must be sold privately, and cannot be offered to members of the public. The main advantages of the private company are that shareholders enjoy limited liability, they are able to obtain more capital, and they are unlikely to suffer from continuity problems. The main disadvantages are that the firm may have to pay corporation tax, and may still have insufficient funds to expand.

Public companies must have a minimum of 7 shareholders, although there is no maximum number. The main advantages are limited liability; the free transferability of shares (shares can be offered to the public); individuals can invest small amounts in companies without taking a part in management. The main disadvantages are that corporation tax has to be paid; and the large number of shareholders may mean that management may effectively control the firm.

Public companies obtain their finance from four main sources.

1. Retained profits.
2. Bank borrowing.
3. **Debentures.** These are loans with a fixed rate of interest, and a redemption date, on which the loan will be repaid.
4. **Shares.** There are two main types of share, ordinary shares and

preference shares. Preference shares earn a fixed rate of interest, and preference shareholders receive their return (called a 'dividend') before ordinary shareholders. Ordinary shares receive a dividend which is dependent upon the company's profits. In a good year ordinary shareholders receive a high dividend in a bad year they may receive nothing.

Co-operative enterprise

A co-operative enterprise is a business organization which is collectively owned by those with a direct interest in the firm. Producers co-operatives exist where the ownership and control of the enterprise rests with those who work in it. Consumers co-operatives are enterprises which are owned and controlled by the consumers of the firm's output. The major advantage of the co-operative is that the enterprise belongs to the producers and consumers and not to some remote shareholders; this will improve the motivation of the workforce. The main disadvantage is that co-operation may be inspired by ideological motives, rather than commercial ones.

Public enterprise

Public enterprise occurs when the state enters into productive activities; in the U.K. this is achieved through the nationalized industries. Public enterprise is responsible for a significant share of the nation's output and employment. The major reasons for nationalization are: (1) To control monopoly power which may be the result of economies of scale, or through the operation of a natural monopoly by private enterprise. (2) To provide capital to infant industries. (3) To manage the contraction of a declining industry. (4) To cover the divergence between private and social costs and benefits. (5) To ensure the security of supplies of a particular good. (6) To aid in national planning.

The main arguments against nationalization are (1) That nationalized industries are so large that they are subject to diseconomies of scale. (2) That nationalized industries have insufficient competition, which would encourage efficiency. (3) That some nationalized industries misuse their monopoly power. (4) That nationalized industries are subject to political interference, resulting in inefficiencies and losses.

Control of nationalized industries

This is achieved through Ministerial control (control by the appropriate Minister), Parliamentary control and the Consumers' Consultative or Advisory Councils.

Chapter 6. Distribution

The distributive trade provides the connecting link between producers and consumers. This is achieved through the Commodity markets, wholesalers and retailers.

The commodity markets provide the link between the producers of raw materials and manufacturers who use these raw materials to produce other goods. Several of the world's commodity markets are in London, although the business is international.

Wholesalers

The distinguishing characteristic of wholesaling is that the wholesaler operates between business units. The main functions of the wholesaler are as follows: (1) They simplify distribution. (2) They hold large stocks. (3) Wholesalers can 'break bulk'. (4) Wholesalers provide an information channel between retailers and producers. (5) Most wholesalers provide at least one specialist service.

Retailers

The characteristic of the retailer is that he acts as a link between a business unit and the final consumer. The major functions of the retailer are: (1) To stock a small quantity of a large range of products. (2) To provide a wide range of services to the consumer. (3) To provide an after-sales service. (4) To provide credit facilities. (5) To advise the wholesaler and the producer regarding customers' requirements. (6) Some retailers provide a delivery service to their customers.

The structure of the retailing trade with respect to ownership identifies several types of retailer.

1. **Independents** are defined as retailers operating up to 9 small establishments. Such enterprises tend to be conveniently located, and often provide a friendly personal service. They are unable, however to buy large quantities and are thus forced to pay higher prices for their produce; this means that they are often more expensive than other retailers.
2. **Multiples** are retail organizations with at least ten establishments. Multiples have tended to specialize in one product area, although there are also 'variety multiples'.
3. **Retail co-operatives** account for about 7% of all retail trade.
4. **Department stores** sell a wide range of products, and encourage shoppers to buy all their requirements under one roof.

5. Other forms of retailing include mail order selling, mobile shops and market stalls, and vending machines.

Recent developments in distribution

The main developments in distribution which have occurred during the last twenty years have been the elimination of the middleman by large retailers and manufacturers, who now carry out the relevant functions. Secondly, the growth of the average size of retailers and thirdly the development of self-service stores.

Advertising

The advertising industry aids the distributive process by providing consumers with information about products. The Advertising Association claims that advertising has several advantages: (1) It increases consumer knowledge. (2) It encourages low prices. (3) It aids the entry of new firms. (4) It increases sales.
The major disadvantages of advertising are that some advertising encourages harmful practices, such as smoking, and raises prices as firms engage in advertising.
The main groups involved in the advertising industry are the advertisers, the advertising agencies which organize advertising on behalf of the advertisers, the media owners such as newspapers which carries advertising, and the specialist ancillary services provided by groups such as graphic artists and film producers.

Hire purchase

Hire purchase or instalment credit enables consumers to buy goods over a period of time, and thus is an important factor in the total sales of expensive consumer durables.

Consumer protection

In the U.K. a wide range of legislation attempts to ensure that consumer's rights are safeguarded and their interests protected.

Chapter 7. Location of Industry

A wide variety of factors influence the decision to locate a plant, firm or industry. These include:
(1) The supply of raw materials. (2) The proximity and size of the market. (3) Transport. (4) The supply of power. (5) The supply of water. (6) The supply of labour. (7) Land. (8) The supply of components. (9) Waste disposal facilities. (10) Government spending policy.

Concentrated and dispersed industries

Some industries are scattered throughout the country and are termed 'dispersed' industries. Other industries are concentrated in particular regions.

The regional problem

The regional problem refers to the regional imbalance in employment and prosperity, mainly due to the decline of the 'older' industries which were highly concentrated in some parts of the country. To attempt to overcome this problem various governments have introduced legislation to try and improve employment opportunities in certain areas – this type of action by government is termed 'regional policy'.

Regional policy

The 1972 Industry Act provides the basis of U.K. Regional policy. Unemployed workers in the areas of high unemployment are encouraged to move to areas where there is work, and financial assistance is available for workers who wish to move. Firms are offered a wide range of financial inducements to locate in areas of high unemployment, at the same time controls on development exist elsewhere.

New towns

Since 1964, 32 new towns have been designated, and they now have a combined population of over 2 million. The new towns have been planned to help the dispersal of the population from the congested conurbations.

Chapter 8. Population

Population can be defined as the total number of inhabitants of a particular place or area. The study of human populations is called demography. The study of population is of great importance, since the population determines both the demand for scarce resources, and the total supply of resources available. Many nations carry out extensive population studies to aid in planning.

Changes in population

Changes in population depend on the birth rate, the death rate, and net migration. The birth rate is the number of live births per thousand of population per annum. The two major factors which determine the birth rate are the number of women of child-bearing age (15 to 44 years), and the number of children born to women during this child-bearing period. The number of children born to each woman is influenced by marriage, the cost of raising children, birth control and abortion, job opportunity for women and government policy.

The death rate is the number of deaths per thousand of population per annum. The main factors which influence the death rate are the standard of living, medical knowledge, and the quality of public health services.

If the birth rate exceeds the death rate it is said that there has been a natural increase in population.

The balance of emigration and immigration is termed net migration.

Theories of population

The first major theory of population was put forward by the Rev. Thomas Malthus in 1798. Malthus believed that the population increased faster than the supplies of food and that this would lead to famine, misery, war and poverty. To avoid this, the birth rate would have to be reduced, specifically through later marriage.

The second major theory of population was introduced by Edwin Cannon in 1888, and is the 'theory of optimum population'. A nation's optimum population is that population where with the existing level of economic resources, output per man is at a maximum. Should the population in a country be either greater than or less than the optimum population, then the standard of living will be lower than that enjoyed at the optimum population level.

The British population

A census of population has taken place in the United Kingdom every ten years since 1801, with the exception of the war year, 1941.

The growth of the U.K. population

The history of the U.K. population can be analysed in four time periods.

1. **Pre 1801.** The population grew very slowly during the Middle Ages, birth rates and death rates were high. The population doubled during the eighteenth century, mainly due to a rise in the birth rate due to improvements in living standards.

2. **1801–1911.** The population doubled in the first half of the century, from 11 million in 1801 to 22·3 million in 1851, and almost doubled again in the second half of the century – to 38·3 million in 1901. The death rate continued to fall, and the birth rate

began to fall after 1881 as families choose domestic expenditure rather than larger families.

3. **1911–1941.** The birth rate continued to fall, due to the use of birth control methods, the death of 745,000 younger men during the First World War and the increased employment opportunities for women.

4. **The post-war period.** During the post-war period the death rate has remained fairly stable. The birth rate has tended to fluctuate widely, and there have been two post-war peaks in births, however the birth rate has tended to fall since 1964, and in 1977 was only 11·6 per thousand. Migration has also effected the population of post-war Britain, with a substantial influx and outflow of population. It is expected that the current trend, of emigration exceeding immigration will continue.

The age distribution of the U.K. population

The age distribution gives the percentage of the population in the working-age group (men 16 to 65, women 16 to 60). Changes in the age distribution can have considerable effects on the standard of living. An ageing population is a situation where the numbers leaving the workforce and entering retirement may exceed the numbers of young persons entering the workforce, and thus a diminishing workforce has to support an expanding dependent population.

The sex distribution of the population

At birth the ratio of males to females is 106:100, but a higher death rate in males means that females tend to exceed males from quite an early age. However, the falling death rate has seen the natural ratio of males to females begin to establish itself in the higher age groups. In 1931 females began to exceed males at the age of 25, by 2001 it is expected that males will continue to exceed females up to the age of 60.

The geographical distribution of the population

In the eighteenth century the British population was primarily located in the areas of good farming land, and the large part of the population lived within a triangle which joined London, Bristol and Norwich. The Industrial Revolution was responsible for a remarkable change in the geographical distribution of the population, as large numbers moved to the coal producing areas, where the new industries of coal mining, iron and steel, textiles and woollens, and engineering were located.

Today, the large proportion of the population live in the South

East, the Midlands and the North West. Almost 80% of the population live in urban areas, and in 1977 6 conurbations had a combined population of over 20 million.

The working population

In 1977 the working population of the U.K. was 26·4 million, which represents about 48% of the total population, and almost 75% of those in the working age group. In recent years there has been an increase in the size of the working population, and much of this has been due to the large increase in the number of married women seeking paid employment. In 1951 only 22% of married women were part of the working population, it is now 50% and is expected to rise to 60% by 1991.

The occupational structure of the population

Since 1900 there has been considerable change in the occupational structure of the population. Employment in the Primary industries (agriculture, fishing, mining) has fallen considerably. Total employment in the Secondary industries (manufacturing) has remained fairly stable, although the distribution of employment within this sector has changed. There has been a movement out of the 'older' industries, such as shipbuilding, and into the 'newer' industries, such as the production of electrical goods. There has been a large increase in employment in the Service (tertiary) industries, particularly banking, education and health care.

World population

The world's population is expanding at a rate of 2% per annum. Some parts of the world, notably Western Europe, have reached a position of population stability, where both birth and death rates are low, and the population is increasing very slowly. However, a second boom in population growth began in the mid 1950s (the first had occurred in Western Europe some 150 years before).

The application of medical knowledge and improvements in sanitation have reduced the death rate, but birth rates remain high, with the result that the developing nations which are experiencing this large increase in population are struggling to feed their populations. Possible solutions to this problem include measures to reduce the birth rate and to increase agricultural productivity as quickly as possible. However, success up to the present has been very limited.

Chapter 9. The Price System

In a market economy, resources are allocated through a system of prices; each price is determined in an individual market by the interaction of the forces of supply and demand.

Markets

A market is a place or an area where buyers and sellers are in contact with one another, for the purpose of trading a particular good or service, and for the fixing of prices.

Demand

Demand is defined as the willingness to buy a good backed by the ability to pay for it. Thus, only 'effective' demand is considered. Demand refers to demand at a particular price, and per period of time. Thus the demand for tomatoes in the United Kingdom might be 500,000 kilos per month at a price of 35 pence per kilo.

Individual demand schedules

It is possible to obtain the demand by individuals for a product. Consumers can be asked to estimate their demand per time period at various prices.

Market demand schedules

It is theoretically possible to interview all the consumers who form an effective demand for a product, and the market demand per time period at various prices can be obtained by adding together the demand of all the individuals.

Market demand curve

The market demand schedule can be represented graphically by a market demand curve. The shape of the market demand curve is downward sloping from left to right, indicating that a higher quantity is demanded at a lower price.

Changes in demand

Demand for a product will change if the conditions of demand change. The conditions of demand are:

The prices of other goods. If the prices of other goods change the demand for another product can also change. If two goods are substitutes an increase in the price of one will increase the demand for the other; if two goods are complements then an increase in the price of one will decrease the demand for the other.

The real income of consumers. If the real income of consumers falls then the demand for all products can normally be expected to fall. On the other hand a rise in real income will normally increase the demand for a product.

Tastes and fashions. If the tastes of consumers change in favour of a good then the demand for it will increase, a change in tastes away from a product will reduce demand.

Population. An increase in population will tend to increase the demand for a good, whereas a decrease in population will tend to reduce demand.

A change in the conditions of demand will either shift the demand curve to the right (if there is a rise in demand) indicating that a higher quantity is demanded at ALL prices, or will shift the demand curve to the left (if there is a fall in demand) indicating that a smaller quantity is demanded at ALL prices.

Supply

The supply of a commodity is that quantity that sellers are prepared to sell at a given price. It is possible to obtain a supply schedule for each individual seller, which relates the price of the good and the quantity that the seller will be prepared to sell at each price per period of time. The individual supply schedules can be added together to obtain a market supply schedule. The market supply schedule can be represented graphically by a market supply curve.

Changes in supply

The quantity that suppliers are prepared to sell at each price will change if the conditions of supply change. The conditions of supply are:

Weather. The supply of many agricultural products is determined by the weather. The supply curve will move to the left if poor weather conditions result in a bad harvest.

Technology. Improvements in technology which reduce costs will move the supply curve to the right.

The cost of factors of production. If these costs rise the supply curve will move to the left, indicating that sellers are prepared to sell a smaller quantity at every price.

Taxes and subsidies. A tax on a good will shift the supply curve to the left by the amount of the tax. A subsidy will shift the supply curve to the right by the amount of the tax.

The prices of other goods. If the prices of other goods rise producers will be encouraged to stop the production of the product in question, and produce other goods (assuming that the higher prices involve higher profits). This will reduce the supply of this product and thus the supply curve will move to the left.

The determination of market price

The market price of a product is determined by the interaction of the forces of demand and supply. At one price, and at only one price, the quantity the sellers are prepared to sell will equal the quantity the buyers wish to buy. This price is called the equilibrium price. If the price in the market is higher than the equilibrium price, sellers will be unable to sell all of their output, and this will induce them to lower the price. If the market price is lower than the equilibrium price sellers will soon sell out, and this will induce them to raise their price. In this way there is a tendency for the price in the market to approach the equilibrium price.

Elasticity of demand and supply

Elasticity of demand is the responsiveness of the quantity demanded to changes in price. If demand is unresponsive to price demand is said to be inelastic; if demand is highly responsive to changes in price, demand is said to be elastic. The main factors which determine the elasticity of demand are: (1) The availability of substitutes. (2) The proportion of income spent on the good. (3) The variety of uses for a good. (4) Whether the good is a habit-forming product. Elasticity of supply is a measure of the responsiveness of supply to changes in price. Supply can be described as inelastic (if supply is unresponsive to changes in price) or elastic (if supply is responsive to changes in price).

Chapter 10. Competition and Monopoly

Economists have devised two limiting cases which describe the extreme conditions of market competition. At one end of the competitive spectrum is perfect competition, and at the other end is monopoly, where there is no competition. Real-life markets lie between the two extremes, some approaching perfect competition and others tending to monopoly.

Perfect competition

Perfect competition is a market situation where: (1) There are a large number of buyers and a large number of sellers. (2) No buyer or seller is large enough to affect market price. (3) The product traded is homogenous. (4) Perfect information is available. (5) There is freedom of entry for new buyers and sellers. (6) Economic friction does not exist.

Under perfect competition, P=AR=MR=MC=AC.

The advantages of perfect competition as a market form are that firms produce at the lowest point on the average cost curve, and this means that inefficient firms will be driven from the industry and economic resources will be used efficiently. Secondly, as there are many small buyers and sellers consumers will benefit from low prices.

Monopoly

Monopoly is a market situation where one firm or individual produces the entire output of a product. Monopolists face a downward sloping demand curve, and thus if the monopolist wishes to sell a higher quantity, then price must be reduced.

The effects of monopoly

Monopoly results in a lower quantity being produced at a higher price than would have been the case under competition. Secondly, the monopolist does not produce at the optimum level of output, and thus resources are not used efficiently. Thirdly, the monopolist may become inefficient as there is no incentive to reduce costs as there is no competition. Sometimes monopolists are more efficient than a large number of small firms operating in a competitive manner.

Forms of monopoly

In theory monopoly exists where a single firm supplies the total output of a product. In practice firms can enjoy monopoly profits even when there are several suppliers, if the suppliers combine to act as a single firm through the use of restrictive practices. The main forms of monopoly are:

1. **The single firm monopoly.**
2. **Local monopolies** may exist for products which are expensive to transport in relation to the price of the good.
3. **Trade associations** in the past have operated a wide range of restrictive practices designed to make high profits for member firms.
4. **Cartels** are selling syndicates.

Monopoly policy in Britain

The government has attempted to control monopoly in the U.K. through legislation relating to the single firm monopoly, restrictive trade practices and mergers.

Major anti-monopoly legislation includes:

The Monopolies and Restrictive Practices Act, 1948.
The Restrictive Trade Practices Act, 1956.
The Resale Prices Act, 1964.
The Monopolies and Mergers Act, 1965.
The Fair Trading Act, 1973.
The Restrictive Trade Practices Act, 1976.

Chapter 11. Wages and Trade Unions

Wages

A wage is a payment made under contract by an employer for the services of labour. The economist includes all payments for labour under the heading of wages including salaries, fringe benefits, bonus payments and payments received through profit-sharing agreements.

Methods of payment

It is common for workers to receive payment through a combination of two or more methods.

Time rates involve payment according to the number of hours worked. The majority of blue collar workers are paid on an hourly basis, their wages being calculated on the number of hours worked. Overtime is usually paid at a higher rate of pay. Time rates have the advantage that workers can concentrate on producing a high quality output, but they do have the disadvantage that as both good and poor workers receive the same payment there is little incentive for workers to work hard. Management may need to employ supervisory staff to ensure that workers produce an output of an adequate quality and quantity. Where it is very difficult to measure output, time rates are the only feasible method of payment.

Piece rates involve payment according to the quantity of work produced, and thus a fast worker will earn more than a slow one. The major advantage of this type of system is that workers are encouraged to work hard to obtain high wages. However, the piece rate system encourages workers to rush, and shoddy work may be produced as a result. Workers may overwork in an attempt to gain high wages, resulting in poor health and a high labour turnover.

Fringe benefits are non-money payments, such as luncheon vouchers, medical insurance and pension schemes.

Profit sharing schemes have been introduced by firms for their workers, and it is claimed that such schemes improve the motivation of workers, reducing industrial conflict and encouraging effort. However, workers may suffer badly if the profit element of earnings is large, and the firm does badly.

Wage rates and average earnings

Average earnings are frequently higher than the wage rate, which is paid for a specified length of working week. Many employees receive overtime payments, bonuses, shift-work allowances and other additions to the basic wage. The difference between wage rates and average earnings is termed **wage drift.**

Wage differences

Differences in earnings between different occupations exist for the following reasons:

(1) Skilled men are likely to earn more than unskilled men.

(2) Higher wages to compensate for dangerous and dirty jobs.

(3) Some occupations involve insecurity of employment, so workers have to be compensated for this through higher wages.

(4) Trade unions may be able to achieve better wages for their members, than for non-unionists.

(5) Social status and the level of monotony will also affect the wage rate for a particular occupation.

Equal pay

The 1970 Equal Pay Act attempts to eliminate discrimination between the sexes with regard to pay and conditions of work. There has been a reduction in the difference between the wages paid to men and women during the seventies, which reflects the effects of equal pay legislation and the changing status of women in society.

Trade Unions

At the end of 1977 there were 461 listed trade unions in the United Kingdom, with a combined membership of 12·7 million. There are four basic types of trade union in the U.K.

1. **Craft unions** represent groups of skilled workers within a particular trade or craft, such as engineers. Wage bargaining becomes difficult when many small unions representing small groups of skilled workers are involved.

2. **General unions** represent large numbers of semi-skilled and unskilled workers from wide areas of industry. Problems can occur if groups within a general union follow sectional interests.

3. **Industrial unions** attempt to organize the workers in one industry into a single body. This simplifies collective bargaining, but problems can occur if groups of workers within the union follow sectional interests.

4. **White collar unions** represent white collar workers, such as teachers, managerial staff, office staff and shop workers. The white collar unions are the fastest growing sector within the trade union movement.

Union organization

The main common characteristics of most unions, with regard to internal organization are:

The branch, which is the local unit of the union, which elects delegates to attend the national conference of the union.

The annual conference is the policy making body of the union. The National Executive is responsible for the day to day running of the union.

The General Secretary is the most important member of the National Executive.

Local bargaining

Local bargaining takes place between management and workers as well as the national negotiations. Local bargaining deals with such issues as level of bonus payments, length and timing of breaks, job allocation and other working practices.

The aims of trade unions

The TUC has distinguished ten main aims of trade unions:

1. Improved terms of employment.
2. Improved physical environment at work.
3. Full employment and national prosperity.
4. Security of employment and income.
5. Improved social security schemes.
6. Fair shares in national income and wealth.
7. Industrial democracy.
8. A voice in government.
9. Improved public and social services.
10. Public control and planning of industry.

The functions of trade unions

Trade unions attempt to achieve their aims in three ways. Firstly, through collective bargaining with employers. Secondly, by attempting to influence government policy. Thirdly, through the provision of certain direct benefits for their members.

Industrial action

Industrial action is used by workers to put pressure on employers when collective bargaining has been unsuccessful. The main forms of industrial action are:

Strikes. A strike is a complete withdrawal of labour by workers. Unofficial strikes are those that do not have the backing of the union. Official strikes are supported by the union, and members usually receive strike benefits. Official strikes tend to be fewer in number, but last much longer than unofficial strikes. The majority of strikes are disputes over wages.

Picketing is an attempt by those on strike to gain the support of other workers either by persuading them to join the strike or by refusing to do the work of those on strike. A work-to-rule is used in those industries where there are a large number of regulations, and where the strict observance of the rules can bring the organization to a standstill.

A go-slow occurs when workers carry out their duties at a slower rate than normal.

The Trades Union Congress

The TUC was formed in 1868, and represents the views and interests of the 112 trade unions which are affiliated to it, and which in 1979 had a combined membership of 11·9 million. TUC policy is determined by the annual conference of the affiliated unions, and a General Council is responsible for the day-to-day running of the Congress.

Chapter 12. Money

Money can be defined as anything which can be used as a medium of exchange or as a measure of value and which is generally acceptable as such.

Barter

Barter is the direct exchange (swop) of goods and services. Barter presents several problems. It is necessary to find someone who is prepared to trade, there is some scope for argument about the rate of exchange, persons with one large product will find trade difficult and it is difficult to obtain a share in the output of a commodity.

The functions of money

1. Money serves as a medium of exchange.
2. Money serves as a unit of account.
3. Money serves as a store of value.
4. Money serves as a means of making deferred payments.

The functions which money performs has several advantages over a barter system:

1. Money encourages the division of labour.
2. Money makes loans and savings easier.
3. Money enables the individual to divide up his resources and wants into very small units.
4. Money is a highly liquid asset.
5. Money is easy to store.

The development of money

The limitations imposed by barter encouraged the use of goods which could be used as a medium of exchange. The major problems with these early forms of money, such as salt and fur pelts, were that they varied in quality, were sometimes bulky and not easily divisible, and they deteriorated. Precious metals like gold and silver overcome these difficulties.

During the sixteenth century, the wealthy began to deposit their gold in vaults, and in return would receive a note promising to pay the bearer a certain quantity of gold. Soon these promisory notes began to be used as a method of payment. The goldsmiths began to issue the notes in convenient denominations, and the general acceptance of paper as a form of money was soon established. The banks realised that they could issue notes with a total face value in excess of their holdings of gold, as only a few people actually required repayment in gold. A series of crises during the eighteenth century led to government control of notes, and since 1921 only the Bank of England has had the power to issue notes in England and Wales. The fractional backing of notes is now commonplace throughout the world and since 1931 it has not been possible to convert bank notes into gold in the U.K. Notes and coins are now legal tender, which means a creditor must by law accept them if they are offered in payment.

Bank deposits

Only about 10% of the value of money transactions are settled by cash. The remaining 90% is settled by cheque. A cheque is a written instruction to a bank to pay a specified amount of money to a person or organization named, from the bank deposit of the drawer. No money need change hands, the deposits of the drawer will be reduced by the amount of the cheque, and the deposits of the person named increased by that amount.

Chapter 13. Inflation

An inflation is an increase in the general level of prices, which results in a fall in the purchasing power of a given sum of money. Inflation has been higher during the 1970s than during any other decade of the twentieth century throughout the world. Inflation is regarded as one of the major economic problems facing the U.K., and the control of inflation has been a major priority of government since the early 1970s.

Measuring inflation

The rate of inflation is measured by the use of a price index. An index of prices attempts to gauge the effect of all price changes by attaching most importance to the prices of those goods on which people spend most money. This is done by 'weighting' each item or group of items; the weight is dependent on the volume of spending on each item.

The Retail Price Index

Changes in prices paid by the general public are measured by the Retail Price Index, which measures the overall change in the cost of a basket of goods, and is expressed in index form by taking the cost of the basket at the starting date as 100. The composition of the basket is based on information from the Family Expenditure Survey which is a continuous survey of the spending patterns of 7,000 households each year. The composition of the basket is brought up to date in January.

Types of inflation

Economists distinguish between creeping inflation, which is a process of gently rising prices of about 2 to 4 per cent per year, and hyperinflation, which is a process in which prices are completely out of control.

The effects of inflation

1. **Redistribution of income.** Inflation redistributes income between members of the community. Those on fixed incomes, and workers who have a weak bargaining position lose out, whereas workers in strong trade unions are able to obtain wage increases to compensate for inflation, and firms can obtain higher profits, and thus dividends will also tend to rise. Debtors will benefit at the expense of creditors, since the real value of loans will fall.
2. **Employment and production.** If the U.K. has a higher rate of inflation than her trading partners, then exports will fall, imports will rise, and both production and employment in the U.K. will fall since there will be a low demand for British products.
3. **The balance of payments.** As imports will rise and exports will fall, if the rate of inflation in the U.K. is higher than in other countries, then this will have a detrimental effect on the balance of payments.

The causes of inflation

1. **Monetary demand pull** inflation occurs when the level of monetary demand in the economy exceeds the supply of goods and services with the result that the prices of all goods rise.
2. **Cost push** inflation occurs when prices rise because firms face higher costs. Higher cost may originate in wage increases, rises in the prices of raw materials, or an attempt to increase profits.

Anti inflation policies

There are two basic policies to attack inflation. To reduce monetary pull inflation a strict control of the money supply is advocated. Cost inflation can be attacked by the use of a prices and incomes policy.

Chapter 14. Banking and Finance

The money market

The money market, which is also called the discount market, is a market for short-term loans, usually of less than three months duration, required by the government and companies. Treasury bills are used by the government to finance its borrowing. Treasury bills are offered for sale to the public, and are sold to the highest bidder. They are usually issued for a period of 91 days.

Commercial bills are similar to Treasury bills, but they are issued by private firms. Discount Houses buy these bills at a smaller amount than the government or company returns to the holder, and the amount paid for the bills determines the rate of interest that the discount houses are prepared to offer.

The Commercial Banks

The main functions of the commercial banks are as follows:

1. They accept deposits to current accounts and deposit accounts.
2. Lending Banks provide loans to private individuals and firms.
3. The banks transfer deposits, as instructed by the written statements of their customers (i.e. cheques).
4. They provide a wide range of services for their customers.
5. The banks create credit. They are able to lend a higher quantity than their assets are able to cover, since only a fraction of deposits held by banks are required in cash.

The Bank of England

The Bank of England was founded in 1694 to manage the government's debt. It was nationalized in 1946. The main functions of the Bank of England are:

1. To issue bank notes.
2. To act as banker to the government.
3. To act as banker to the commercial banks.
4. To manage the country's monetary system for the government.

Monetary control

Monetary policy is used by the government to influence the level of economic activity. This is achieved by controlling the cost and availability of credit, through the influence that the Bank of England has over the commercial banks and other financial institutions. The main methods used are:

1. Open market operations.
2. The special deposit system.
3. Minimum Lending Rate.
4. Funding.
5. Direct controls.

The capital market

The capital market provides long-term loans to firms to finance fixed investment. The sources of long-term capital are examined in detail in Chapter 5.

The Stock Exchange

The Stock Exchange provides a central efficient market for second-hand stocks and shares. The main value of the Stock Exchange is that it encourages investors to buy new issues, in the knowledge that these can be resold on the Stock market.

Ways of saving

The savings of individuals, firms and institutions can be directed to manufacturing and commercial enterprises, which provide circulating and fixed capital, and earn a rate of interest for the investors.

The main methods of saving are listed below:

(1) Commercial banks. (2) Building Societies. (3) National Savings. (4) The Trustees Savings Bank. (5) Shares in public companies. (6) Government securities. (7) Finance Houses. (8) Unit Trusts and Investment Trusts. (9) Insurance companies and Mutual societies. (10) Local Authority bonds.

Chapter 15. National Income

National income is the total output of goods and services produced in an economy over a period of time, normally one year, and represented in money values. There are three ways of calculating national income: (1) The Income method. (2) The Output method. (3) The Expenditure method.

(1) The Income method

The calculation of the national income using the income method is achieved by adding together all the incomes received from domestic production. Transfer payments are not included. An account is made of property income from abroad, to achieve 'national product'. Capital consumption is subtracted since this represents those goods which have been used up during production.

(2) The Expenditure method

This method involves the summation of all expenditures on domestically produced goods and services. Since some goods and services are exported, exports must be added, but since some expenditure in the U.K. is on goods and services produced abroad, imports must be deducted. A further problem arises with taxation, since the summation of all expenditures will include the effects of indirect taxation and subsidies. Thus to negate these effects, indirect taxation is deducted and subsidies are added.

(3) The Output method

This involves the summation of the total output of all domestic producers. However, to avoid double counting a value added approach has to be used.

The use of national income statistics

The national income statistics can be used to measure changes in the national income, although some account must be made of the effects of inflation, and changes in population. International comparisons can be made, although fluctuations in exchange rates can cause problems.

Chapter 16. The Public Sector

In 1977, the state employed 28·5% of the U.K. workforce. Total Government Expenditure was £61,964 million, which represented almost 45% of the Gross National Product. This expenditure was financed mainly from taxation – £51,095 million.

Government expenditure

The reasons for government expenditure are:

1. The provision of public goods.
2. The provision of social services.
3. To increase industrial efficiency.
4. To influence the level of economic activity.

The structure of public expenditure

Since 1945 government expenditure has increased as the state has widened its responsibilities. The changes that have occurred in the structure of public expenditure have been a reduction in the proportion spent on defence, trade and industry, and an increase in spending on the social services.

Public revenue

Taxation is the major source of public revenue. The main objectives of taxation are:

1. To raise revenue.
2. The management of the economy.
3. The redistribution of income and wealth.
4. To influence specific expenditures.

The principles of taxation, as laid down by Adam Smith in 1776 are (1) Equity. (2) Certainty. (3) Economy and (4) Convenience. Taxes are often classified as either direct or indirect. A direct tax is levied on income, capital, property or wealth. An indirect tax is levied on spending.

The structure of taxation

There are three main types of taxation, taxes on income, taxes on capital and wealth, and taxes on spending. The main taxes on income are Income tax, Corporation tax and Petroleum Revenue Tax. The main taxes on capital are the Capital Gains Tax, Capital Transfer Tax and Development Land Tax. The main taxes on spending are Value Added Tax, Rates, and a wide range of customs and excise duties.

The Budget

The Budget is the legislation which arranges the raising of tax for the following financial year, and is also the occasion on which the Chancellor of the Exchequer describes the economic policies which the government intends to follow during the year.

Budgetary policy

If the government decides that public spending is to exceed revenue from taxation, the budget is described as a deficit. If taxation exceeds spending it is termed a budget surplus, and if taxation and spending are equal, it is termed a balanced budget.

Chapter 17. International Trade

Nations specialize on the procution of those goods and services for which they have the greatest advantage over other countries. A proportion of output may then be exchanged for other goods and services produced by other countries.

The basis of trade

A nation may enjoy either a 'natural' or an 'acquired' advantage over other countries, enabling it to produce a particular good or service more cheaply.

The gains from trade

By specializing in the production of those goods and services which it produces best and trading any surpluses, the nations of the world could, theoretically increase the total output of each and every good. In a real world the gains that countries can obtain from this are limited by transport costs and the need that is felt by many countries that there are certain vital commodities that it must produce internally even if the good could be bought more cheaply elsewhere.

The terms of trade

The rate at which goods of one country exchange for goods of another is given by the terms of trade, which is the ratio of the index of export prices over the index of import prices.

Restrictions on trade

Nations place artificial barriers which restrict trade, the main forms of restriction are:

1. Tariffs. A tariff is a tax on an imported good.
2. Quotas. A quota is a quantitative restriction on the imports of a good.
3. Exchange controls.
4. Subsidies to home produced goods.

Arguments for protection

The main arguments for protection are:

1. To raise revenue.
2. To protect declining industries.
3. To protect infant industries.
4. To ensure a secure source of supplies.
5. To aid the balance of payments.
6. To reduce general unemployment.

The General Agreement on Tariffs and Trade (GATT) was established in 1947 and tries to reduce the barriers to trade, and thus encourage world trade.

Britain's overseas trade

In 1977 Britain was the fifth largest trading nation in the world. Four-fifths of Britain's exports consist of manufactured goods, whereas imports consist of mainly raw materials, finished manufactures, and food beverages and tobacco. Britain's main trading partners are the members of the EEC, other Western European countries, North America and the Oil exporting countries.

The Common Market

Britain joined the European Community on 1 January 1973. The Community consists of three separate communities with a single administration, the European Coal and Steel Community, the European Atomic Energy Commission and the European Economic Community.

Chapter 18. International Payments

The main difference between internal trade and international trade is that different countries use different currencies.

The balance of payments

The balance of payments is a table which shows the financial transactions of the U.K. with the rest of the world. It is organized into four main sections.

1. The current balance is obtained by the summation of the visible balance (the exports and imports of goods), and the invisible balance (the exports and imports of services).
2. Investment and flows of capital are recorded under the heading 'investment and other capital flows'.
3. The balancing item is the net effect of errors and omissions.
4. The total currency flow is the sum of 1, 2 and 3 above.

Exchange rates

A rate of exchange is the price of one currency in terms of another. Exports create a demand for the pound, but British imports create a supply of the pound sterling on the foreign exchange market. If imports exceed exports, then the supply of pounds will exceed the demand and the price of sterling will fall, providing that the country operates a system of freely fluctuating exchange rates. If a system of fixed exchange rates operates, then the U.K. government would have to raise the price of the pound on the foreign exchange market by demanding pounds and selling foreign currencies. The fixed exchange rate system has the advantage that government action of this type keeps the exchange rate stable, and encourages international trade. However there is a limit to the extent that a nation can continue to support its currency in this way, and thus many nations prefer a system of floating exchange rates, which enables a currency to find its own value in the free market.

The International Monetary Fund was set up by the Bretton Woods agreement of 1944, to act as the central organization of the world's monetary system. Although the world has since changed from a system of fixed exchange rates to a system of floating exchange rates the IMF still holds its place, and strives to encourage the expansion of international trade through a system of stable exchange rates.